For Mama and Daddy

Table Of Contents

Introduction

Someone once told me that every preacher really only has one sermon. We may preach it seven times seventy different ways, but one is all we preach. If that's so, I'd like to think the title of this little book is what my people hear week after week. **The Lord is Risen!** He is risen indeed! **He really is!**

The title comes from the sermon I've included for Easter Day. For a number of years I've had the privilege of preaching at four masses the week after Easter at the St. Charles Roman Catholic Church in Lima. They have been most gracious and have come to expect, as has my own congregation, that my Easter messages always begin the same way: **The Lord is Risen!** Neither congregation has many, if any, who remember anything else I said. But they remember that **The Lord is Risen!** Maybe that's enough.

At first glance the Easter title may seem somewhat out of place on a book half full of sermons for Lent. As my own writings say, Lent is a time for introspection, retrospection, and close inspection of ourselves in preparation for the Easter message. Some of the lessons for Lent seem to have less to do with a risen Lord than with a fallen Dick Sheffield. Somehow contrasting my failings with the fantastic message of Easter is supposed to make Easter more meaningful. There is no doubt some truth in that. But I think the greater truth, that we serve a risen Lord, is the one truth we should proclaim in every season of the year and every season of life.

The Rev. Dr. Donald Macleod, professor emeritus at Princeton Theological Seminary, is one of many who have taught me that. Dr. Macleod was known by students for being incredibly particular, if not downright punctilious, about matters related to preaching and worship. But you didn't have to agree with him on everything to respect his high standards, or to be his friend. Don hammered into my head the difference between the prepositions "in" and "of." The Sundays during Lent are "in" Lent, he would say, NOT "of" Lent. Sunday, even during Lent, is the Lord's Day, and the Lord's Day, as in the understanding of our Puritan forebears, is a "little Easter" every week. Without a doubt Don is right both theologically and liturgically. He is also right mathematically. Lent is traditionally a forty-day period, finding its length in Jesus' forty days in the wilderness. But if you count, starting with Ash Wednesday, the first day *of* Lent, you will find that there are actually 46 days 'til Easter. The extra six days are the Sundays which fall *in* or during Lent, but are not liturgically part *of* it.

In a day and age when all kinds of language issues are raised in the life of the church, on the assumption that language matters, surely it matters that every time we Christians gather on the Lord's Day, even "in" Lent, that we proclaim amidst all our teaching and singing that **The Lord is Risen!** I have tried in the sermons that follow.

I should note that the sermons that follow are not a "sermon series." They were all preached before a "live" congregation in the midst of living out its life in a particular place at a particular time. That place is Lima, Ohio. They were preached over several years. Their common thread is my life and the life of the congregations I have served, and, I hope, their one voice proclaiming our risen Lord.

With the gracious consent of the good folks at CSS Publishing Company, these sermons have not been altered to remove all personal, or even community references. They are not generic. And they are not really preachable right out of the book. I don't know how to preach that way. Should anyone want to preach one of my efforts more-or-less "as is" I would be flattered. And I suppose that with substitution of personal experiences or other local community concerns that could be done. If that would be of any help during one of those weeks we all have, do it with my blessing! And let me know how it went. I won't tell.

Thank you to our church secretary, Pat Mooney, who takes my texts and publishes them weekly in the church *Newsfold*. Thank you to the whole staff at the Market Street Presbyterian Church who protect my time for preparation when I will let them. Thank you to my editor, Terry Rhoads at CSS, who is also a member of my congregation and listens to me before she edits me. (She does both kindly!) Thanks to my family for putting up with my preacher's schedule — and with me. Thank you to everyone who's ever taken time to listen. I hope you've heard **The Lord is Risen!** That's really all I'm trying to say.

Richard L. Sheffield
September, 1997

Lent To Life

Matthew 6:1-6, 16-21

Ash Wednesday is the first day of Lent. A Sunday school teacher asked her class if anyone could tell her what Lent is. One especially precocious little boy piped up, "Sure. It's what you get when you clean your bellybutton."

So, it's in BIG letters on your bulletin: L-E-N-T, Lent.

And today is the first day of Lent. We call it "Ash Wednesday," even though few, if any of us, have ever actually done as our Catholic friends do on this day and been marked with the ashes of repentance in the form of a cross on our foreheads.

We Protestants aren't too big on that sort of stuff. But I thought for moment earlier that that was about to change. (I looked around. Some of you did too!) John Wurster spoke thoughtfully and seriously about ashes and their representation of our creation from the earth and our eventual return to it.

He brought to mind the words spoken at grave side, "Ashes to ashes, dust to dust," ALL THE WHILE standing right there in the center aisle holding a plate of ashes that I now know he got from his fireplace. I questioned John about that, and John said, "Well, you know, ashes are hard to come by." It's true. Especially in a Presbyterian church. Marking ourselves for all to see as less than we should be and not nearly what we could be isn't one of our favorite things. Is it?

Even though the truth be known we know the truth about ourselves, the truth about our lives — we just wait 'til death to say it: *earth to earth, ashes to ashes, dust to dust.*

I read recently of a funeral director who signs all his correspondence, "Eventually yours." Eventually, he's right. And whether we show it or mark it on Ash Wednesday, we know it.

Many of us may have the same question as little Johnny. The story goes that:

> On their way home from attending an Ash Wednesday service, little Johnny asked his mother, "Is it true, Mommy, like the minister said? We come from dust?"
>
> "Yes, darling," his mother answered, probably hoping he wouldn't ask any more questions about where he came from!
>
> "But is it true, Mommy, that we go back to dust again when we die?" (That's the question none of us want to ask.) "Yes, dear," his mother replied.
>
> "Well, Mommy, when I said my prayers last night and looked under the bed, I saw someone who is either coming or going." [1]

Life's like that, isn't it? We're caught, coming and going. Like dust — under a bed. Blown about by every breeze. That's why we laughed. That's also why we have Lent. A time of reflecting on life, reorganizing the priorities of life, recognizing the path our life is on, reconnoitering the possibilities of the life that's still before us. A life full of lint — and this once-a-year cleaning season we call Lent.

Lent means literally, "lengthening days," and points us toward spring. I don't know if you've noticed but the days *are* getting longer. Today is two minutes longer by the sun than yesterday. But have you also noticed that in those same small increments, life is getting shorter, for you and me? The "end of the world," a matter of much speculation (and much nonsense) as we approach the turn of the millennium, whether it comes with the explosion of a meteor crossing our orbit, or with a whimper in two or three billion years, will come *for you and me* within our life-time. The end of the world will come all right. But not in some God-caused catastrophic event. God is about re-creation not wrecking creation. The end of the world will come — when you die. Because life only gets shorter and because death only gets nearer, we have Lent. A time of disciplined reflection on our often undisciplined lives.

But contrary to popular piety the disciplines of Lent are not meant to make us wish that this time in our life would be quickly over, so we can get on to something else. Rather, a disciplined Lent is meant to make all the times of our lives, the time of our life, time we pray will last forever.

In the lesson from Matthew that the lectionary assigns for Ash Wednesday, the disciplines of Lent are laid out by Jesus himself. Not as a matter of "liturgy" but as a way to live. Actually those are the same thing. "Liturgy," in its original meaning, simply means "the work of the people." What people do. How people live. Worship reflects the rhythms of life. Life should be worshipful. Jesus lays out a way of life worth living.

The lesson from Matthew describes a life worth living in terms of giving, praying, and fasting. Giving to others in a way that gives glory to God and not just credit to you. Praying so that God can hear you, not just so others can. And fasting, a spiritual discipline unfamiliar to most of us that simply means learning by experience what you can live without. But doing it in such a way that it isn't intended to gain the sympathy of others for poor, deprived you. The bottom line of such a life is that it is God-serving, not self-serving.

In such a life, giving becomes more than another way of getting. (Though those I know who give this way get more than you can imagine in return.) Praying becomes listening to God, instead of just expecting God to listen to us while we list things for him to do. Fasting becomes a way of keeping things simple and avoiding being drowned in life's trivialities.

There are worse ways to live. Like the way a lot of us live. What Lent is about is learning to live a life worth living forever.

So this Lent let's look at our life and how we live it; our time and how we tend it. This Lent, let's look for better ways to live better.

This Lent, let's give up giving up, and learn to give to others and to each other what God has given to us. Let's make the best of

13

our life. Let's learn to live — like Lent leads to life. Like Lent really does lead to Easter.

1. *Holy Humor: A Book of Inspirational Wit and Cartoons*, eds. Cal Samra and Rose Samra (Thomas Nelson, 1997), p. 36.

Lint

Matthew 4:1-11

The topic this morning was not a misprint in the newspaper nor
in your bulletin. The topic is "L - i - n - t" — as in belly-button.

"Lent," L-*e*-n-t, is the season just before Easter when for forty
days, excluding Sundays, we remember Christ's forty days in the
wilderness (as described in the Gospel lesson this morning). "The
primary focus is not on giving up one or two of life's minor plea-
sures, but rather on rededication of ourselves to the Christian life
as a preparation for the Easter Season to come. Personal sacri-
fices, instead of being ends in themselves, become means by which
we put our whole existence under scrutiny, reject those things that
have drawn us away from Christ, and refocus our lives with Christ
as the center. Lent is a time for introspection, for slowing down
our helter-skelter existence, for times of quiet questioning."

I got that straight from the front page of last week's *Market
Street Newsfold*. The newsletter of the First Presbyterian Church
in Findlay brought a slightly different focus: in an article titled
"Remember, You Are Dust." The article talks about the centuries-
old tradition of "Ash Wednesday," the first day of Lent, and the
smudge of ash placed on the forehead of many Christians to the
words, "Remember, you are dust."

Terry Bard notes that many of us shy away from that, thinking
of it as a curse, or judgment. It's not only "Catholic" (whatever we
mean by that), it's unsettling to be reminded of our mortality. Yet,
says Terry, the point is not curse but reassurance. He quotes Dr.
Walter Brueggemann who wrote: "Human persons are dependent,

15

vulnerable and precarious, relying in each moment, on the gracious gift of breath which makes human life possible ... God knows our frame, God remembers that we are dust. (And) remembering that we are dust, God reaches out to us in 'steadfast love.' "

The two newsletters together suggest that Lent should be a time of "quiet questioning" about the way we live in the reality of our mortality. What we do with the life God has given to us. A life whose reality is summed up well in the title of a meditation by William Leety of Covenant Presbyterian Church in Scranton, Pennsylvania, writing in *Presbyterian Outlook*. The title is "Desert Shield, Desert Storm, now Desert Jesus." *Jesus* in the desert of life is the subject of Lent. Leety writes: "Somehow the battle with God or with Satan seems mild now when set alongside scuds and tanks, barbed wire and boredom, fear and fatigue."

But the story of Jesus' time in the desert is told to remind us that in *our* time in the desert, be it in the desert of Saudi Arabia, or in the desert of our soul, God remembers that we are dust and reaches out to us in steadfast love.

That story of Jesus' time in the desert is actually a lot closer to our contemporary time in the desert than you might think.

Saddam Hussein is what Jesus would have become if he had succumbed to the devil's temptations.

Each of those offers us a sermon in itself.

The devil said, "Make bread from stones. Be completely self-sufficient, control your own destiny, *take* what you want whenever you want." Hussein says, "Yes!" Jesus says, "No!"

Well, at least *do* what you want, (said the devil). Claim God is on *your* side, instead of praying that you are on *his* side.

Put God to the test! Make him prove he's on your side! Hussein says, "Yes!" Jesus says, "No!"

Well then, *be* what you want (says the devil). Look at the kingdoms of the world, and take them for yourself. Worship power and you shall be powerful. Hussein says, "Yes!" Jesus says, "No!"

Jesus always says no to these very human temptations. Lent is the time to look at ourselves to discern the times when *we* say *yes* to temptation and the enemy we face in the desert is us. We become our own worst enemies when life is simply, *take* what you want, *do* what you want, and *be* what you want without regard for others and our God.

With that as our Lenten agenda, we'll need forty years not forty days. In fact, I've already had forty years and I'll need forty more to deal with all that. So let me suggest you start with the "Lint." L- i-n-t, the little stuff that gums up your VCR, and your life.

L-*e*-n-t is from a word meaning "lengthen" or "lengthening days." The promise of spring. L-*i*-n-t suggests the need for a bit of spring cleaning in our lives. Getting the lint off our lives.

Too many of us, though, do the opposite. We visited Disneyworld a while back, and I've been intrigued to learn that they have a staff in charge of lint, or more accurately, dust. And I don't mean to clean it up and maintain their squeaky clean image. I mean to manufacture it and load it on in the haunted house. The way so many of us load it on in our haunted lives. The official Disneyworld book says, "For Disney maintenance crews (the Haunted Mansion) is a veritable nightmare. To keep it nice and dirty furnishings must be constantly covered with dust and covered with cobwebs. 'Dust' is purchased by the pound and distributed like grass seed from hand spreaders; yet it seems to evaporate into thin air. Legend has it that since the Magic Kingdom opened in 1971, maintenance personnel have spread enough dust to *bury* the Haunted Mansion."

In addition to the big stuff, too many of us load on piles of the little stuff. We work at it and wonder why life is dusty and dingy and dreary and dry and dead.

Two things to help clean house: 1) Give up giving up; 2) Give up gossip.

Give up giving up on yourself and on God. A lot of stuff we *need* to give up, but too many people I know give up on themselves and on God. They assume life won't work and they work hard to prove it; and find out they're right. The only thing easy in life is taking it easy — giving up; we do it too easily.

I read an article recently on how easy it is to decide that something is impossible. You might call this the "lint" of history: Simon Newcomb, speaking at the turn of the century: "Flight by machines heavier than air is unpractical and insignificant ... utterly impossible." Or this: "We don't like their sound. Groups of guitars

17

are on their way out." That was the management of Decca Recording Company in 1962 as they turned down the rights to record an unknown pop music group called the Beatles. And watch what you say to kids. A German schoolteacher said to a ten-year-old pupil: "You will never amount to very much." Little Albert was Albert Einstein. What if Orville and Wilbur, or Paul, George, John, and Ringo, or little Albert had given up?

That article concluded: "Why can *some* people accomplish the impossible while others cannot? The major factor is faith, the faith that this impossible feat should, must, and can be done. To that kind of faith, you simply add three other ingredients: creative thinking, hard work, *and the unwillingness to give up*. God does the rest."

Jesus was tempted, more than once, more than just that first "Lent," those first forty days after his baptism, and had every good reason but he never gave up. Get the lint off. Give up giving up this Lent!

And second, Give up gossip. That may sound like a new subject, but it isn't. Gossip is the favorite hobby of those who have given up on others and on themselves. Jesus says we are to live *"by every word that comes from the mouth of God."* Too many of us die "by every word that comes from the mouth of someone we thought was a friend." **Gossip is saying about others what you feel about yourself.** Now that everybody knows that, watch what you say about yourself to others.

A newsletter from a friend's church in Brooklyn, New York, brought this story: "There was a peasant with a troubled conscience who went to a monk for advice. He said he had circulated a vile story about a friend, only to find out the story was not true. 'If you want to make peace with your conscience,' said the monk, 'you must fill a bag with chicken feathers, go to every door in the village, and drop in front of each one a fluffy feather.' The peasant did as he was told. Then he came back to the monk and announced that he had done penance for his folly. 'Not yet,' replied the monk, 'take up your bag, make the rounds once more, and gather up every feather that you have dropped.' 'But the wind must have blown them all away,' said the peasant." So it is with words. They are easily dropped, but no matter how hard you try, you can never get them back again.

If you want to teach that to children so they'll remember, use the words of the theologian in the movie *Bambi*. Thumper the Rabbit learned this from his mama: "If you can't say sumpin' nice, don't say nuttin' at all."

Jesus knew everything about everybody. He was tempted but he never gossiped. Give up gossip this Lent! Instead, live as the famous writer "unknown" put it:

> *Promise yourself to be so strong that nothing can disturb your peace of mind. To talk health, happiness, and prosperity to every person you meet. To make all your friends feel that there is something good in them.*
>
> *Promise yourself to look at the sunny side of everything and make your optimism come true. To think only the best, and to expect only the best.*
>
> *Promise to be just as enthusiastic about the success of others as you are about your own. To forget the mistakes of the past and press on to the greater achievements of the future. To wear a cheerful countenance at all times and to give every living creature you meet a smile.*
>
> *Promise to give so much time to the improvement of yourself that you have no time to criticize others. To be too large for worry, too noble for anger, too strong for fear, and too happy to permit the presence of trouble.*
>
> — Adapted from the "Optimist's Creed"
> written by Christian Larson

It's **Lent**.
Get the **lint** off and **live** in Jesus Christ.

The Stealth Disciple

John 3:1-17

In the "Science & Technology," section of a recent issue of *Business Week* magazine, there was an article about the latest on A - I - D - S, the complicated disease we've come to know simply as AIDS. It says the scientists are learning a lot. One of the things they're learning is how the disease kills. And like just about everything that matters, it isn't simple. Says *Business Week*, "... HIV doesn't mysteriously lie dormant in the body only to emerge years later, as once thought. Rather, the virus goes on the attack from the very start, making up to a staggering ten billion copies of itself a day. (In essence, they're saying once infected you fight it every day for the rest of your life.) Yet confronted with this pernicious assault, the immune system does manage to keep the upper hand for years — sometimes even a decade or more.

"Scientists now believe that dramatic gains could be made by providing the body's natural defense with a little help early on. 'This is the most hopeful thing to come out in years,' says Dennis M. Burton of Scripps Research Institute. 'The virus is not a sinister thing waiting to hop out. Instead, it wins just by grinding you down.' "[1]

I've had this article on my desk and I kept reading that last line to myself, 'til I decided this week to read it to you. "The virus is not a sinister thing waiting to hop out. Instead, it wins just by grinding you down." Substitute "evil" for "the virus." *Evil is not a sinister thing waiting to hop out.* (Like a bogey man under the bed.) *Instead, it wins just by grinding you down.*

Speaking of love, which is more the opposite of evil than of hate, the Apostle Paul wrote, "**Love** is patient; love is kind; love is not envious or boastful or arrogant or rude. It does not insist on its own way; it is not irritable or resentful; it does not rejoice in wrong-doing, but rejoices in the truth" (1 Corinthians 13:4-6 *NRSV*). Says Paul, "**Love** is patient ..." Say the scientists, the HIV virus is patient. **So is evil.** It wins " ... just by grinding you down." Wearing you out. Making your patience wear thin. Evil is not just something we do battle with — win or lose — today or tomorrow. It is something we live with every day of our lives. Some of us are victims of AIDS. All of us are victims of EVIL. It lurks like a virus to which none of us is immune. And more often than any of us want to admit, it wins, just by grinding us down. It isn't so much the evil that comes upon us unexpectedly, but the evil we've come to expect — and maybe accept — that does us in.

The article in *Business Week* is titled "Bob Gallo's New Weapon Against AIDS." You might entitle the passage I just read from John's Gospel, "God's Old Weapon Against EVIL." "For God so loved the world that he gave his only Son, so that everyone who believes in him may not perish but may have eternal life," said Jesus (John 3:16). God's weapon, God's way of dealing with evil, is God's love. Love, which Paul has defined first-and-foremost, in a long list of things love is, as **God's patience** with you and me. Whatever else love is, God's or yours or mine, it is patient in dealing with the day-to-dayness of the evil that chews us up and grinds us down.

Sometimes I wish God weren't so patient with this or that person. I wish God weren't so patient with this or that situation. When I wish that, I have to remember sometimes that God is also patient with me! The HIV virus' patience is what makes it deadly. The patience of evil is what grinds us down. God's patience is God's love.

And God's *intention* for you and me is the orphan verse of the third chapter of John. It's "orphaned" because its cousin, John 3:16, gets all the play. It even gets played up at football games by fans flashing large cardboard signs. I'm waiting for someone someday at some game to hold up a big sign that reads JOHN 3:*17*! So when the television audience breaks for a beer, they can grab a

Bible and read:

> "... God did not send the Son into the world to condemn
> the world, but in order that the world might be saved
> through him."   — John 3:17 *(NRSV)*

> "... God did not send his Son into the world to condemn
> the world, but to save the world through him."
>   — John 3:17 *(NIV)*

> "God did not send his Son into the world to condemn its
> people. He sent him to save them!"
>   — John 3:17 *(CEV)*

We have to be careful lest we suggest, by holding up John 3:16 alone, he really sent him to "sort-us-out." Save a few good ones for heaven, and send the rest to hell. That's NOT what it says. *You can send yourself to hell*, and many of us do day-by-day. God sent Jesus to save us from the hells we build day-by-day for each other and for ourselves. From the evil within and without that grinds us up and wears us down.

That's what Jesus was trying to say to Nicodemus. As Marion Soards puts it, "Jesus declares that humans must be born 'from above' — that is, by the power of God renewing their lives. Humans need to be 'born anew,' but in the sense of rebirth by God's power at work in their lives rather than merely being born 'once more.' "[2]

Soards goes on, "Unfortunately, Nicodemus is not the only one who fails to grasp Jesus' meaning, for many in the world today cheerfully use the language of Nicodemus' misunderstanding to describe their theological conviction that they are 'born again.' "[3]

What Jesus had to say to Nicodemus had less to do with the one-time conversion of one person, and more to do with the conversion of all life for all time to be "... on earth as it is in heaven." And it has nothing to do with judging "... the validity of a person's faith ... by whether one has been 'born again.' "[4] It was, in fact, such judgments about others, out of misreading or misunderstanding or misuse of God's word, that Jesus so often condemned.

23

Nicodemus was a Pharisee, a good and learned man. He knew the rules. He lived by the rules. He also judged others by the rules — while, as he perceived it, Jesus didn't. He perceived it right. Jesus knew the difference between right and wrong but no difference between "me and thee." He treated the worst of us along with the best of us as children of God. But that isn't how a lot of good people saw things — or saw Jesus. They saw someone who repeatedly broke the rules as they believed them.

So, perhaps that's why Nicodemus came at night. Just being seen with Jesus could be seen by some as breaking the rules. I think of Nicodemus as the "stealth disciple." He swoops in by cover of night and is "gone again" within a few verses. He is not seen or heard from again in the Gospels until Jesus is dead and John tells us Nicodemus helped bury him. Describing that scene, John's Gospel says simply, "Nicodemus, who had at first come to Jesus by night, also came ..." (John 19:39).

Nicodemus had come as we all come — in the darkness of our lives. But Nicodemus also came in the living of his life to see the light of truth in Jesus Christ. Nicodemus lived the words that Isaiah wrote of a dark time in the life of the people of Israel, "Those who walked in the dark have seen a bright light. And it shines upon *everyone* who lives in the land of darkest shadows" (Isaiah 9:2 *CEV*).

That's what God wants for you and me. God does not want for you or me condemnation and he does not condemn us. To be condemned already (as the passage says) does not mean simply that God is chief "judge and executioner." But rather without faith, defined as the life-giving spirit of God, we are condemned to life in which death wins just by grinding you down. And not just death but dying daily. It isn't that God will get us later. What gets us is what's grinding away right now.

But Nicodemus didn't get it. The conversation between Jesus and Nicodemus sounds like an argument between an obstetrician and a theologian. Nicodemus is talking about birth as we know it, and being born again, while Jesus is talking about being born anew, renewed by the power of the one who knows how old this life we're born into gets sometimes.

Unlike other instances Jesus doesn't tell Nicodemus to go do good or go be good or even to go be generous. So, let's you and me be generous. Assume Nicodemus was already doing all that. Jesus is saying it isn't enough. Not that it isn't enough for God, but that it isn't enough for Nicodemus — or you — or me. Nicodemus seems to sense that. Otherwise, why does he come to Jesus in the dead of night? Why, if not to seek a life worth living during the day? Nicodemus said to Jesus, Sir, I see you do miracles. Jesus said to Nicodemus, I see you need to be born from above. Nicodemus said to Jesus, C'mon — no one can be born again! "How can a grown man ever be born a second time?" (John 3:4 *CEV*). By this time Nicodemus was probably saying to himself that he should've stayed home in bed. He came looking for a straight answer and Jesus gave him ambiguity.

The word in Greek is: *anothen*. Born again. Born anew. Born from above. Nicodemus wanted to be told what to do now. Jesus wanted him to think about what he would do for the rest of his life. He couldn't be born again. He couldn't go back and start over. But he could start now to be renewed and made new by God above. Jesus wanted Nicodemus to believe not just because of the miracles, what Jesus could make happen now, but because of the difference real belief would make in renewing his life. He wanted Nicodemus to believe in the reality of God's goodness and mercy in the reality of our lives.

The emphasis is not on whether he will or he won't (be born anew) but rather on how that has to happen. Jesus' emphasis is on "born from *above*." Something God makes happen. Not something we make happen with the right doctrines, the right words, or even the right prayers. Jesus said to Nicodemus, "... only God's Spirit can change you into a child of God" (John 3:6 *CEV*). Nicodemus no doubt had been taking care of that himself. He believed the right doctrines. He kept the right rules. Even prayed the right prayers. And presumed that made him right with God. And there are those running around who've made that approach to Christianity into a growth industry in our day.

There isn't much new! But Jesus said to Nicodemus, "Only God's Spirit gives new life" (John 3:8 *CEV*). And, "God's Spirit is like the wind that blows wherever it wants to." (You can't turn it on and off with your television remote.) "You can hear (it) ... But you don't know where it comes from or where it is going" (John 3:8 *CEV*). You can experience it, you can feel it, you can be touched by it, you can be challenged by it, you *will* be changed by it, but you cannot control it. Bad news for any of us who qualify as "control freaks." As my wife Xavia once wrote,

> *One of Life's greatest successes*
> *is to lose control of others*
> *and gain control of yourself.*
> *Life's greatest success*
> *is to give control of yourself*
> *to God.*
> — Xavia Arndt Sheffield

That is essentially what Jesus was saying to Nicodemus. But Nicodemus was clearly an early Presbyterian. He responded, "How can this be?" To which Jesus responded "How can *you* be ..." (John 3:10 *CEV*) everything that you are, and still not get it?

That's a good question. One we need to ask often. With all that we are, and all that we do, do we get it?

Martin Luther called Jesus' words to Nicodemus, words to help him "get it," "the gospel in miniature." The most succinct way of putting it, so everyone could get it, Martin Luther wrote:

> *Did we in our own strength confide,*
> *our striving would be losing;*
> *Were not the right Man on our side,*
> *the Man of God's own choosing.*
> *Dost ask who that may be? Christ Jesus, it is He,*
> *Lord Sabaoth His name.*
> *From age to age the same,*
> *and* He *must win the battle.*[5]

J. B. Phillips put it this way: "For God loved the world so much that he gave his only Son so that everyone who believes in him should not be lost, but should have eternal life. You must understand that God has not sent his Son into the world to pass sentence on it, but to save it — through him."[6]

Get it?

Then go live like it.

Go love like it.

Go let God *be* God in your life, and live a life worth living — forever.

John suggests that eventually Nicodemus got it. That God loved him. God loves us!

Do we get it?

_____

1. *Business Week,* January 15, 1996, p. 87.

2. Marion L. Soards, *Scripture and Homosexuality: Biblical Authority and the Church Today* (Louisville, Kentucky: Westminster John Knox Press, May 1, 1995), p. 8.

3. *Ibid.*

4. *The New Interpreter's Bible, Volume IX,* John (Nashville, Tennessee: Abingdon Press, 1995), p. 554.

5. Martin Luther, "A Mighty Fortress Is Our God," *The Presbyterian Hymnal,* no. 260, stanza 2 (Louisville, Kentucky: Westminster/John Knox Press).

6. *The New Testament in Modern English,* J.B. Phillips.

Water, Water, Everywhere

John 4:5-42

Reading the Gospel lesson this week a snatch of poetry I learned somewhere along the way kept running through my head. It goes:

> *Water, water, everywhere*
> *And not a drop to drink!*

I think that's how a lot of us feel a lot of the time. The song we'll sing in a few minutes says, speaking to God:

> *See, the streams of living waters,*
> *Springing from eternal love,*
> *Well supply thy sons and daughters*
> *And all fear of want remove.*
> *Who can faint while such a river ever flows their thirst to*
> *   assuage?*
> *Grace, which like the Lord the giver,*
> *Never fails from age to age."* [1]

Sounds good. We sing it, and then from the depths of our souls we say, "So?" So where is it? So when do I get it? So why do I feel like the Ancient Mariner?

> *Water, water, everywhere*
> *Nor any drop to drink.* [2]

Why is life so dry?

Why am I so thirsty in the midst of so much?

You can put that question in the poetic context of Coleridge's epic story of the seafaring man, the ancient mariner, who *"... shot the Albatross."* A man who took dead aim at life itself and discovered too late that he'd shot himself. And then found himself at sea, surrounded by water as far as he could see, that he could not drink, because to do so was to die. Salt water makes you want more water and more salt water will kill you.

You can put things that way, or you can take the more modern approach and think of our human dilemma as being adrift on a sea of things that the advertisers tell us will satisfy our every need, our every want, our every thirst. When they're really like salt water. Once tasted they leave you wanting more — and more — and more — until you die.

We should have learned by now that you need more than "more" to find meaning in this life. But somehow life comes like an albatross, "a bird of good omen," that gets shot dead in the living of it. We take on life but often feel like we got took!

The poet wrote,

> *God save thee, ancient Mariner!*
> *From the fiends, that plague thee thus! —*
> *Why look'st thou so?" —With my cross-bow*
> *I shot the Albatross.*[3]

And so our Prayer of Confession this morning says: *"Please save us from ourselves, we pray through Christ."*

The last time I read *The Ancient Mariner* some teacher made me. It was an assignment. As I re-read it this week it spoke to me, as Jesus spoke to that woman at Jacob's well. A well where tradition had it there had been water since the time of Jacob — for nearly 2,000 years!

Whether John intends for us to understand the well in a literal sense, a place where you could put down a bucket in the desert and draw up water, or the well is symbolic of the wellspring of our faith in the faith of Abraham, and Isaac, and Jacob — whose name became Israel — whichever way you take it, Jesus said to the woman, it is not enough, this water. Faith in what always has been here will not do. And faith in the faith of others is not enough.

Or, maybe more positively, because Jesus clearly valued the faith of Israel, Jesus said to the woman, "Woman, there is more." There is more to life than your day-in-and-day-out trips to this well for water. There is more to life than the mundane living of life. There is more to life than the mess your life is in. There is more that God has to offer, and he offers it to you as surely as you can offer me a drink of water, Jesus said to the woman.

Jesus was tired. He was human. And he was hot. "It was about noon" (John 4:6 *NRSV*). The disciples were off running errands. Jesus was sitting by the well. He had the same human needs you and I have. And that day he needed a drink of water. The woman came to do what she had to do every day. And he asked her for one. "... Jesus said to her, 'Give me a drink' " (John 4:7 *NRSV*).

What isn't so obvious is that by asking for water Jesus was asking for trouble. Jewish men did not talk to unknown women. Jewish teachers did not talk to any woman in public. And Jews in general did not talk to Samaritans. Jesus did.

That "astonished" his disciples, it says (John 4:27 *NRSV*), and apparently amazed the woman. " 'You are a Jew,' she replied, 'and I am a Samaritan woman. How can you ask me for a drink of water when Jews and Samaritans won't have anything to do with each other?' " (John 4:9 *CEV*). Literally, "Won't use the same cups,"[4] in the same way that white folks and black folks wouldn't use the same water fountain at Kress' 5 & 10 store where I grew up.

Well, Jesus would. In fact, he would do far more than that, as she soon found out. He offered her something more than what he asked. He offered her what he called "living water." He knew that all the water in that desert water hole would not meet the woman's need for meaning. No matter how many times she came to fill her bucket.

Scottish theologian William Barclay once wrote that "... there are two great days in a person's life, 'the day we are born and the day we discover why.' "[5] The woman needed more than water to stay alive. More than just to continue the fact of her birth. She needed the meaning that comes with knowing why — that makes life worth living. So Jesus offered her not a magic potion to cure all her ills, but the elixir of life itself.

In desert lands where making it from one water hole to the next water hole was and is a matter of life and death, water is a symbol for life. Modern slang says, "Get a life." Jesus says, I've got a life to give to you. He was talking to her as he also talked to Nicodemus — about having a life worth living forever.

She heard him wrong. How can you give *me* water! You don't have any way to get it! You can't even get your own! You have no visible means by which to do anything about my thirst. My thirst for the water in this hole in the ground, or my thirst for meaning and wholeness in my life!

One author says, "... Jesus' words about living water seem preposterous to her, empty boasts by a man without a bucket."[6]

Jesus' response is that the water she draws from the well sustains day-to-day life; and what she can do she's done; but the water he's offering gives life forever, and makes day-to-day life worth living, and only he can do that.

The woman said, "Gimme," but she still didn't get it. Not the water. The point. Somehow she understood that having drunk this water the day-to-day living of life would be taken care of. All her problems would be over. This is a mistake you and I make when we assume that following Christ means not having problems, instead of what it really means, which is having help in the problems every one of us has.

The woman had problems. And Jesus knew it. Jesus knew she'd had five husbands. Jesus knew the man she was living with was not her husband. It sounds like a Hollywood script. But maybe not. The fact that we make assumptions about the woman's morality based on her marital situation is not supported by the story. And what we assume may tell us more about ourselves than about her!

She may have been caught in problems not of her own making. Sometimes we are. It's possible that all those husbands simply died. And that the man who by their custom should have then married her and taken care of her — the next brother in line — refused.

She may have been a widow five times over with no way out but to live with whoever took her in.

A woman in that society had few choices. She may have been what we would call a victim of circumstance. Something that's true of all of us sometimes. (Not all the time — but sometimes.) Life just isn't the way we intended it to be — and neither are we. We are like the Apostle Paul who wrote: "The good I want to do — I don't do; and the bad I don't want to do, I do." No matter how hard we try "that's life"!

When that is life, it's helpful to take note of the fact that Jesus just stated the facts about the woman and her life. He did not judge her. **He did not condemn her!** Instead he kept his offer open. An offer still open to you and to me. For living water. To be made alive by the presence of God in our lives. To discover that in life as God intends it to be, there's

> *"Water, water, everywhere,"*
> **and plenty enough**
> **to drink and share.**

---

1. John Newton, "Glorious Things Of Thee Are Spoken," *The Presbyterian Hymnal, No. 446* (Louisville, Kentucky: Westminster/John Knox Press).

2. Samuel Taylor Coleridge, "The Rime of the Ancient Mariner," Part 2, Stanza 9.

3. *Ibid.*, Part 1, Stanza 21.

4. John 4:9 *CEV*, note.

5. Source unknown.

6. *The New Interpreter's Bible, Volume IX*, John (Nashville, Tennessee: Abingdon Press, 1995), p. 567.

Blind Driveways

John 9:1-41

King George VI, addressing his subjects at the beginning of a new year, said in his annual message: "I said to the man who stood at the gate of the year, 'Give me a light that I may tread safely into the unknown.' And he replied: 'Go out into the darkness, and put your hand into the hand of God. That shall be to you better than light, and safer than a known way.' "

The Gospel story is about a man who all his life had tread in physical darkness — but put his hand into the hand of God and could see. And it is about Pharisees — rejoicing people — who had their sight — who, we soon find out, were treading in spiritual darkness — and pulled away from the hand of God.

We start out in sympathy for the physically blind man — and the question that the disciples raised. Why is he so handicapped? What has been done to deserve such a fate? But we end up with sympathy for the spiritually blind Pharisees — and maybe, still the question: Why? Why would those so learned, who could quote the Scripture word for word — why would those be so blind?

The story about the blind man is not primarily a miracle story about healing ... or at least the restoration of sight to the blind man is the least of the miracles. It's really a story about spiritual sight — about vision — and how it grows and nurtures us — or how it eludes us. The storyteller intends to remind us that it isn't what we see physically that makes life good or bad. With minor adjustments for bifocals we all see the same things. Even Helen Keller, blind from birth like the man in the story, "saw" the same things we see — with different senses, but just as clearly. Perhaps more clearly.

Because it's a matter of what we see in what we see that dictates how we experience life. The blind man saw Jesus. The Pharisees saw Jesus. One saw a healer, a savior, a friend. The other saw a Sabbath breaker, a sinner, a threat to be dealt with. How they responded to Jesus depended on what they saw in Jesus.

Herman Hollerith saw something in a thing that everyone else had seen that has determined the life direction of our whole society. Hollerith was an engineer who helped compile the 1880 United States census. (Market Street Church was already fifty years young!) It took seven years of tedious clerical work to gather the data and tabulate the information. Hollerith was looking for a better way. One day, while riding on a train, he noticed the conductor punching holes in a railway ticket to record the bearer's destination and the fare. On many trains they still do it the same way.

But do we see what Hollerith saw? Using what he saw, Hollerith designed a punch to be used by census collectors to record a person's vital statistics by means of holes in a card. The cards were then read with an electromagnet. Because of this punch card invention, the census in 1890 took half as long and cost $5 million less. Because of what Herman Hollerith saw in what everybody else saw — you and I can now see the possibilities of life in ways he never imagined, as we turn our electron microscopes to see the world within and our shuttle-borne telescopes to see the worlds beyond. What Herman Hollerith saw on the train became your desktop computer.

Sometimes there is a block to our seeing. Certainly we would say the Pharisees had one. A while back, I was driving along a road, trying to stay slow enough to avoid the speedtrap I knew was there. Then I rounded a curve and saw a sign I'd seen hundreds of times before. It said: "Blind driveways." You see them often on curvy roads. On the Ohio driver's test they expect you to know the signs. "Blind Driveways" doesn't mean that the driveway is blind, but that the circumstances of the road make you or me blind to the driveway. It says pay attention. There's something there you don't see; there is a block to your seeing. The Pharisees said to Jesus: "Surely we are not blind!" We know the way. Jesus said to them: "If only you *were* blind, then you would not be guilty of sin. But now that you claim to see, your sin remains." Pay attention! The warnings are up. It's a blind curve. There's something unexpected going on here. You think you see. You don't see!

Sometimes in life we need to take a new look at things — at signs we've seen before — and God may use our circumstance to make that happen. That's what it means when it says, "The man was blind so God's work might be revealed." His circumstance, blindness, was to be turned in God's will into his circumstance of spiritual as well as physical sight. His perspective as well as his physical circumstance was to change.

I like the story of Charles Eliot, the President Emeritus of Harvard University, who used to summer in Northeast Harbor, Maine. Kendrick Strong says that one day, in his ninetieth year, Charles Eliot "made his way down the road from his cottage to the cottage of his neighbors, the Peabodys. Mrs. Peabody greeted him and took him into the living room. After a brief chat, Eliot asked if he might hold her new baby. Mystified, she lifted her infant son from his crib and laid him in Eliot's arms. Eliot held the baby quietly for a few minutes. Then, with a little gesture of thanks, he returned him to his mother, explaining, 'I have been looking at the end of life for so long that I wanted to look for a few moments at its beginning.' " I've been looking at too many signs saying "blind driveways," I want to see around the curve beyond the signs.

Charles Eliot could do nothing to change the circumstance of old age, but he could do a lot about his perspective on life — about how he chose to see his place in life, and the signs along the road. Jesus came that you and I might see beyond the blind driveways and the curves of life.

There is a danger in seeing. It's that we think our insight (the thing we see) is *the* insight (the thing everyone should see). We're all guilty of this. We settle on our laurels, on some key insight, about God and our neighbor, as though we had unlocked all of God's truth for us, and everybody else. But Elbert Hubbard said: "The recipe for perpetual ignorance is be satisfied with your opinions and content with your knowledge." To assume that you have seen all that God desires to show you. That you can ignore the "blind driveway signs." But the story suggests that no matter how much you have truly seen, the moment you make the assumption you've seen it all, you become profoundly blind.

John sets up his story in two scenarios to make the point: The blind man and the Pharisees are depicted as "passing in the night" — one to the light — the other to greater darkness. The blind man by degrees moves from one level of sight and insight to another: he receives physical sight. He acknowledges that his benefactor was the man they call Jesus. He confesses Jesus as a prophet. He defends Jesus before the Pharisees, saying, "He is of God." And then he acknowledges Jesus as "The Son of Man" and worships him.

The Pharisees on the other hand move from one level of blindness to another: at first they accept the miracle of healing but debate the propriety of healing on the Sabbath. Then they doubt the miracle and interrogate the man's parents, seeking to prove he was never blind. Then they seek to trap him in cross examination by having him repeat the details of the story. Finally, those judging the miracle find themselves judged by Jesus himself. As Raymond Brown puts it: "Three times the former blind man, who is truly gaining knowledge, confesses his ignorance. Three times, the Pharisees, who are really plunging deeper into abysmal ignorance of Jesus, make confident statements about what they know."[1] About what they see!

The story is a parable of life into which Jesus came, saying, "I came for judgment, that those who do not see may be able to see, and those who do see may become blind." "I came to give sight to the blind, and to make their blindness apparent to those who think they see!" The man did not claim to have seen God. Only one sent from God. The Pharisees threw him out. When Jesus heard about his expulsion, he found him and said, "Do you believe in the Son of Man?" He answered, "Who is he, sir, that I may believe in him?" Jesus said: "You have seen him."

---

1. Raymond E. Brown, *The Gospel According to John I-XII* (Garden City, NY: Doubleday and Company, Inc., 1966), p. 337.

Upon Those In The Tombs Bestowing Life

John 11:1-45

In the Orthodox Church, Easter worship includes the singing of a hymn that goes:

> *Christ is risen from the dead,*
> *trampling down death by death,*
> *and upon those in the tombs bestowing life.*[1]

I thought of those words this week as I was driving north to Michigan to attend the funeral of a long-time friend — something that seems to happen with increasing frequency as I grow older. Some of you know what I mean. Once I got past the ice and snow on Route 30 going toward Fort Wayne, and onto a dry interstate highway north and could relax and think a bit about where I was going and why, those ancient words came to mind:

> *Christ is risen from the dead,*
> *trampling down death by death,*
> *and upon those in the tombs bestowing life.*

In our Presbyterian tradition, we call the funeral "A Service of Witness to the Resurrection" (*Book of Common Worship*). Because we Presbyterians believe, as do our Orthodox brothers and sisters, that

> *Christ is risen from the dead,*
> *trampling down death by* (his) *death,*

39

and upon those in the tombs
(the tombs where we lay our dead,
and the tombs where we too often live)
bestowing life.

The one in the tomb on Thursday was my friend. The one in the tomb in the Gospel lesson from John this morning was Jesus' friend. Jesus' friend was named Lazarus. Lazarus' sisters, Mary and Martha, had sent word to Jesus earlier, saying: "Lord, he whom you love is ill" (John 11:3 *NRSV*). Apparently with the expectation that Jesus, who had a growing reputation as a healer, would come and heal his friend.

But Jesus didn't come. And Lazarus died. So Jesus set out, as I did on Thursday, but by the time he got there Lazarus had been dead four days. That little detail intends to tell us that Lazarus was really dead. Lazarus was not in a coma. Lazarus was not just critically ill. Lazarus was dead. The details demand it. He had been dead four days. Jewish tradition at the time had it that "... the soul lingered near the body for three days, so that death was truly final on the fourth day."[2] It had been four days. So medically and traditionally, Lazarus was dead.

Jesus' response to that reality was first to reassure Mary and Martha. He said to Martha, who was clearly put out that Jesus had arrived too late to heal Lazarus, "Your brother will rise again" (Luke 11:23 *NRSV*). That is the sort of thing you or I might say to comfort a family at the funeral home. She took that to mean what you and I mean: that in the end those we love will live again — someday.

Not all Jews believed that. Martha did. But Martha also clearly understood — probably better than we do — that death undoes what God has done; unmakes what God has made, destroys what God has created. It's not a transition. It's an end. But Martha also believed that what God had made God would remake. God made Lazarus and gave him life. God would remake Lazarus and give him life again "... in the resurrection on the last day." What the creed calls "the resurrection of the body."

When all is said and done, Lazarus will live. But for now Lazarus is dead. That is underlined for you and me by the writer of John, who reports that when Jesus got to the tomb and asked that it be opened, Martha responded, inelegantly, "Lord, already there is a stench, because he has been dead four days" (John 11:39 *NRSV*).

The Bible never flinches in face of the reality of death, but the Bible is also reassuring as Jesus was for Mary and Martha. Death is real. But those who die will not be dead *forever.* Jesus reassured Mary and Martha of the reality of their faith in the resurrection of the dead.

Then Jesus reacted as all of us do at the death of someone we love. "Jesus wept" (John 11:35 *KJV*). We all do, one way or another, when death comes close. Some of us cry our tears — others of us swallow our tears, a few of us try to deny them, or we are denied them by the way we've been taught. But inside or out, consciously or not, we weep. It's a normal, physiological response to the pain of death. To the separation from someone who in some way is part of ourselves.

"Jesus wept," has often been called the shortest verse in the Bible. A favorite of the children who pick it to memorize. And it is. At least in King James English. But those two words, "Jesus wept," contain within them all kinds of feelings of frustration, and sorrow, and even anger. And as Granger Westburg notes, in his book *Good Grief,* "... these feelings are normal for every human."[3] It was normal and natural *and very human* for Jesus to grieve at the death of his friend; for Jesus to weep. As those around him observed rightly, his weeping was a measure of his loving. "See how he loved him!" they said (John 11:36 *NRSV*).

But they also said something else that caused Jesus to be "greatly disturbed" (John 11:37 *NRSV*). "... Some of them said, 'Could not he who opened the eyes of the blind man have kept this man from dying?'" (John 11:38 *NRSV*). Why is he here now? Where was he, when we needed him? The fact that Jesus didn't do what they wanted him to do led them to blaming him for what happened.

So it was with tears in his eyes, and hurtful words in his ears, "... that, Jesus ... greatly disturbed, came to the tomb" (John 1:38 *NRSV*). Jesus had responded to his close friends Mary and Martha with loving reassurance. Jesus had responded to his own grief with his tears. Now Jesus responded to death itself with his words:

"Lazarus, come out!" (John 11:43 *NRSV*). And Lazarus did. And "Jesus said to them, 'Unbind him, and let him go' " (John 11:44 *NRSV*). Take off those grave clothes and let him live.

In my own life I have been reassured, and have tried to be reassuring when death has come. I have cried, and grieved, and encouraged the crying and grieving of others. I have learned the hard way, which is the only way, how to do that. And so have you. I've been there. We've been there — many times. So, I cannot begin to imagine the shock, the dismay, the incredulous reaction of those around Jesus that day, when they heard his words. "Lazarus, come out! Lazarus, come back to life! Lazarus, be alive! Lazarus, live!"

If Lazarus hadn't walked out about then, they'd have written Jesus off as a lunatic. As having lost his mind. But they couldn't do that. Lazarus was alive. Instead, some of them called a meeting and plotted to put Jesus to death.

It's an interesting omission that there is not one word in the story about rejoicing that Lazarus had rejoined the living. Rather there is no word from Lazarus, and only a word or two about some of them believing in Jesus, and a meeting at which some of them plotted to kill Jesus, because whatever he was doing and however he did it, it threatened the way they wanted things done. The giving of life was perceived as a threat to be met with death.

Charles Cousar writes, "There is not much rejoicing at the raising of Lazarus. Since the giving of life projects a future full of surprises, it turns out to be a menace to those who think they control the future. They respond the only way they know, with violence. They even plot to do away with Lazarus (12:9-10).

"But the larger story confirms that life will not be overcome by death. What remains beyond the raising of Lazarus is not only Jesus' death, but his resurrection and his persistent giving of life."[4]

What remains beyond the raising of Lazarus is the resurrection of Jesus Christ. And those two things are different. Lazarus was raised to live and die again. Jesus was resurrected to live and reign forever. A friend of mine says it's the difference between "resuscitation" and "resurrection." At most, "resuscitation" means a return to life still limited by death. "Resurrection" means return to life unlimited. Life forever. Life where there is no death. Life where death does not control the way we live. Life which is the joyful thing God made it to be.

The promise of the Bible is not simply being brought back to life to face death, but being given life forever so we can face death unafraid.

I said Lazarus didn't have much to say on being raised back to life. He didn't get a book contract or talk show appearances, the way some who claim to have been there and back do in our day. I surmise he was the same old Lazarus, but maybe with a new sense of the wonder of life and the joy to be found in it, because the next time we hear about Lazarus, he's at a party (John 12:1-2), enjoying the company of another party-goer, his good friend Jesus, and heeding, perhaps, as we all should, some old words of wisdom from the rabbis: that God will hold us most responsible after death for the good things in life we refused to enjoy.

Too many of us live by the dictum that if I live a worthy life now, I'll get a life worth living — later. But it's a lie to call that the whole truth. The truth is life now is forever, and it's worth living now, in a way you'd want to live forever. Says the song:

> *Christ is risen from the dead,*
> *trampling down death by death,*
> *and upon those in the tombs bestowing life.*

The tombs where we lay the dead, and the tombs where we live daily, are opened by Jesus Christ who says to you and me — come out AND LIVE! The life he bestowed on Lazarus is the same life he has bestowed on you and me. Life now. And living it well is living as though we will live it forever. Without fear. With full assurance, even in grief, of the love of God in Jesus Christ.

Some of you need to stop there. You may. But I'm not done.

As I was traveling north on Thursday I listened a lot to the news, about life in our world. Four-and-a-half hours each way with news every half-hour. I was thinking about the story of Lazarus and why Jesus raised him, brought him back to this life. And in the context of that, while I was thinking about that, I heard no less than fifteen or twenty times in nine hours of driving, the story about congressional attempts this past week, to repeal the ban on certain types of assault weapons.

I don't make political comments often up here. So bear with me. And if you disagree with me, forgive me. But I need to say this. The contrast between the giving of life in the story from the Gospel, and the dealing in death in the story on the news was jarring.

Assault weapons have one use: deliberate, deadly, assault — on life. On the lives of human beings, like you and me — and Lazarus. I'm no pacifist. And I'm not all that naive. I know those weapons have their place, albeit it a limited one, as the lesser of evils in a too often evil and threatening world. But for the life of me, as I was driving along and listening to the radio, I could not imagine Jesus holding an assault rifle out to Lazarus as he came out of that tomb. Saying, here Lazarus. Welcome back to life as it really is. Where ordinary people need an AK47 or an UZI in the family room. I pictured Lazarus looking wide-eyed at Jesus and saying, "Been there, done that." And heading back for his grave.

Life is not meant to be such that anyone needs an assault weapon, much less wants one. And for the life of me I cannot understand why politics means that's the way it could be again for you and me and our children and our grandchildren. The congress and the National Rifle Association should be ashamed of what they are trying to do. The story of Lazarus says it's wrong. As dead wrong as death itself. That God calls forth life, not death. But the story in the *Lima News* recently calling the vote a "conservative curtsy to the NRA,"[5] said that's the way life is.

It won't be always.

Because

> *Christ is risen from the dead,*
> *trampling down death by (his) death,*
> *and upon those in the tombs*
> be they literal or just the places where we hide, upon us
>   all)
> ***bestowing life.***

44

1. *The Divine Liturgy according to St. John Chrysostom*, copyright 1967 by the Russian Orthodox Greek Catholic Church of America, second edition (South Canaan, Pennsylvania: St. Tikhon's Seminary Press, 1977), p. 179.

2. *The Harper Collins Study Bible*, Luke 11:17 note.

3. Granger E. Westberg, *Good Grief* (Philadelphia, Pennsylvania: Fortress Press, 1971), p. 50.

4. W. Brueggemann, et al., *Texts for Preaching, A Lectionary Commentary Based on the NRSV — Year A* (Louisville, Kentucky: Westminster/John Knox Press, 1995), p. 227.

5. *The Lima News*, Lima, Ohio, 3/23/96.

Where Is God
When I Need Him?

Matthew 26:14—27:66

"Truly, this man was God's Son!" (Matthew 27:54 *NRSV*).

"Truly, this man was a son of God!" (*Ibid.*, alternate reading).

"This man really was God's Son!" (*Ibid, CEV*) said the soldier, at the foot of the cross, as Jesus died.

So where in heaven was God while his Son hung there between heaven and hell; between life and death? Between the hosannas and the hallelujahs — the triumphal entry on Palm Sunday, the not so triumphal exit come Friday — and Jesus' triumphant return to life on Easter — where was God?

The simple, straightforward, orthodox answer is this:

Right there in front of everyone.

Right there; riding on a donkey, receiving the adulation of an expectant crowd.

That's where God was.

Standing before the Roman Governor receiving the third degree.

Rejected by rabble-rousers who called for the release of a man called Jesus Barrabas, instead of Jesus called the Messiah.

Scorned by the powers that be, for whom his activities meant a change in the status quo and in the equation of political power.

Beaten barbarically by soldiers who were "just following orders."

Paraded through the streets of the City a second time, this time not on the back of a donkey, but with a big piece of wood on his back.

Put upon, spat upon, and finally hung upon a cross. Not a decorative cross like ours in the sanctuary, but a deadly cross, the only purpose of which was to kill as deliberately and demonically as you or I could imagine.

That's where God was that week. That week we call "holy," because of what happened — but a week more ghastly than good. That week that begins hopefully today, descends to the depths of hopelessness by Friday, and ends with a new beginning and new hope as the first day of a new week became the eighth day of this "Holy Week," with the resurrection of Jesus Christ.

God was there. For everyone to see.

Hanging on for dear life on the back of a donkey.

Hanging onto life itself in a politically charged situation that finally demanded his death.

Hanging on a cross.

That's where God was.

We need to pay attention to that before we get to next Sunday with its emphasis on where Jesus wasn't. He wasn't in his grave. Come next Sunday.

But that's next Sunday. This Sunday, called "Palm Sunday" because they waved palm branches as he came into Jerusalem; and "Passion Sunday," because people waving palms quickly gave way to soldiers wielding whips; this Sunday we need to ask where God was while Jesus was "descending into hell." Where is God when my life is hell? Where is God when I need him?

We need to ask that, and pay attention to that, because otherwise we end up with what I call "pogo stick" theology. Boinging down on Palm Sunday long enough to enjoy the parade, and then bouncing over to Easter long enough to enjoy the flowers and the fun; without ever coming down to that other reality in between.

But miss the middle and you miss the point. Miss the mess in which Jesus quickly found himself, and you miss the meaning of Easter.

Just about everyone missed it the first time around. And we still do. The crowd missed it that Palm Sunday. They celebrated the way we celebrate: in anticipation of getting what they wanted — in their case, a "messiah." One who would take up the role of king and lead them to freedom from the rule of the Roman Empire. Here was someone they would follow into battle, to fight the "evil empire" of the Roman government, to free themselves from tyranny.

If Jesus had gotten off the donkey and yelled, "Charge," many of them would have. They'd have charged the governor's headquarters with its cohort of Roman soldiers, and died for the right to be free of Roman rule. From time to time during the history of the Jewish people, they did just that. And many in the crowd that first "Palm Sunday" were itching to do it again.

They were remembering, perhaps, as only the Jews can remember, events of just 150 years before when a revolt had been led by one "Judas Maccabeus." The story is in that part of the Bible we call the "apocrypha," the books that lie between Old Testament and New Testament times. My study Bible describes "... Judas Maccabeus as the ideal Jewish warrior — one who prays before battles and gives thanks afterward, always careful to observe the Sabbath and other Jewish rituals."[1]

The crowd was curious. Could Jesus be like him? The crowd was hopeful. Maybe he will be like him. When it became clear that he wasn't like him, the crowd deserted Jesus for someone else, asking, instead of mercy for Jesus who had healed their sick and held out hope of a new way of living with friends and enemies, for the freedom of one called Jesus Barrabas.

It is the same name, according to the best manuscripts. Jesus Barrabas, Jesus Messiah. Or just plain, Jesus — both of them. Our word "Jesus" is really Joshua in anglicized Hebrew. *Yeshua*. A name that means "Yahweh is salvation." "God saves." The answer to the cries of "hosanna," meaning "save us," is the name of the one on the donkey, "Jesus," which means "God saves."

God was there, from donkey to death, but few could see it. What they would soon see clearly was that the Jesus on the donkey would not "save them" the way they wanted to be saved — would not lead a military revolt, or a mob-based uprising against Rome. So given the choice, they chose one, perhaps, who would; who in God's name, his own name, would give them what they wanted.

I've always wondered about the seemingly arbitrary choice of "Jesus Barrabas" as the people's choice. Why a criminal? Perhaps, because to them he wasn't a criminal! The *King James Version* of the Bible simply calls him a "prisoner." Prisoners are bad people. Right? So why this bad guy, Jesus Barrabas, over the good guy — Jesus of Nazareth?

Maybe it's a matter of perception. Barrabas was a bad guy in the eyes of Rome, so he was in a Roman prison, but maybe he was a good guy in the eyes of fellow Jews. The translators of the *Contemporary English Version* of the Bible call Barrabas a "well known *terrorist*" (Matthew 27:16 *CEV*). Exactly the kind of guy to do what Jesus wouldn't. If Jesus won't, maybe Barrabas will! Maybe the people got exactly what they wanted, while missing what they already had. Not just someone named "God is salvation," who goes on to do things his way, Jesus Barrabas; but the God who comes to save, Jesus Christ, who goes his way on a donkey doing good. And when that wasn't good enough — getting crucified for it.

They crucified him! Something most political pundits of the day could no doubt have predicted. Jesus was up in the polls on Palm Sunday, but down in his grave on Friday. That week was like a political primary — Barrabas won, God lost. They crucified Jesus — called the Messiah — the Christ. They crucified him. A word that means death by being nailed to a cross, that has come to mean in our day political or social death by being nailed — by being persecuted and accused of things unfairly.

Back to my original question. Where was God in all that? More importantly, where *is* God in all that? Things are not all that different today. Where *is* God now?

God is where he's always been: with us in all that. In the midst of all our hopes and dreams, even when they turn into despair and nightmares, God is still with us in Jesus Christ. As surely as God was present on that donkey that first Palm Sunday, he is present with you and me on this Palm Sunday, and is ready to go with us into the week to come.

The story of Holy Week is not about God waving a magic wand, but about God walking the walk — the *via dolorosa*, the way of sorrow, the way of life, with you and me.

This week is about God's presence in your life and mine, assuring us, and when necessary reassuring us, that whether it's hope that dies, or one we love who dies, or even ourselves who must die, death does not defeat life in the end. For in the end, as in the beginning, God is there. God is here, to guarantee it.

Most of you know the popular poem called "Footprints." I see it often in memorial folders as people try to make sense out of death — or at least be reassured it's not the end.

It's a little sentimental, but it's become a sort of Psalm for our day, a piece of poetry for those times when prose won't do.

It tells the story of a man looking back over his life and seeing it as a walk along a beach. Looking back along the beach he's walked (the life he's lived), he sees two sets of footprints. His and God's — side-by-side. God walked with him in his life.

But looking closer, he noted some times in his life where there was only one set of footprints. When the walker was alone. He knew *he* was there. It was *his* life. And it was at those times in *his* life that were hardest that the second set of footprints disappeared.

So he prayed to God — as Jesus might've prayed — *did* pray on the cross, as you or I might pray sometimes: Where were you, when I most needed you? Where are you now? Why have you forsaken me? What's this having to walk alone?

To which God replied, my child, when there was only one set of footprints, they were mine. I was carrying you.

The old spiritual says, "Jesus walked this lonesome valley...." This lonesome valley is life as you and I live it. God lived it too, in Jesus Christ. Holy week was a lonesome time, as people turned against him, denied knowing him, and finally abandoned him.

So there is only one set of footprints from today to Easter Sunday. The footprints of Jesus Christ, God himself, who in this holy week, begun as he was carried into Jerusalem on a donkey, got off the donkey and walked alone, carrying you and me.

---

1. *The Harper Collins Study Bible,* 2 Maccabees "Contents," p. 1691.

Go Love!

John 13:1-17, 31b-35

It's late. Let's get right to it. It was late that first Maundy Thursday. Too late. Too late for Jesus to do much of anything except send Judas off to do what he had to do. Jesus told him to get to it. Jesus said to him: "Do quickly what you have to do" (John 13:27 *NRSV*). "Judas, go quickly and do what you have to do" (John 13:27 *CEV*). It's late. Get to it.

My topic this evening is what this Maundy Thursday really is all about. Which is what being a Christian is all about. Which is, when you get right down to it, what life is all about. What Maundy Thursday is all about is not just what Judas did, but what Jesus said. Jesus' commandment: not just to **be** good or **do** good, though for some of us that would be a start; and not just to believe the right things, or pray the right words; not even just to get ourselves "saved," but to do as Jesus said, as Jesus commanded, as Jesus mandated (hence "Maundy Thursday," "Mandate Thursday.") It is about Jesus' mandate, Jesus' command: Do the one thing that's harder than anything else to do — to love. "I am giving you a new commandment (said Jesus). You must love each other, just as I have loved you" (John 13:34 *CEV*).

C'mon, preacher, that's not hard! No? Then you tell me: Why did Jesus think he had to order us to do it? I know we love some of the people some of the time. But all of the people, all of the time, seems to be the standard Jesus sets. He wasn't saying, just "love the lovable," or even "love the likable." He just said love!

Jesus wasn't saying anything new to his disciples. They'd heard it before. Back when someone asked Jesus which of the Ten

Commandments was the most important commandment, Jesus responded with the primary importance of all the commandments. God gave Moses ten. I've seen cartoons where Moses tries to negotiate and get God to give a little; perhaps knowing how little chance we have of keeping all of them, all of the time. Jesus said, ten too many? Fine! One commandment. One word. LOVE!

Not "like." LOVE!

Not "live-and-let-live." LOVE!

Not "look the other way." LOVE!

Not "let-well-enough-alone." LOVE!

Not the eleventh suggestion, but the first and foremost commandment: Thou shalt LOVE!

No choice.

No argument.

No debate.

No compromise.

No wiggle room. LOVE!

And not as Hollywood loves, but as God loves.

It's as though late on that last night with them before his death Jesus cut to the bottom-line for life and death and you and me. Before it's too late, he said: "Love one another!" Like it or not, it's the only way to live. The next day, Good Friday, a lack of love took his life. A lack of love will take your life away from you. Jesus came that you and I might have life. The way to have it is to love.

A few years ago our stewardship commitment slogan was the question: What does love require? That's the question you and I ought to be asking about now. What does Jesus mean when he commands us to "love"? He means what our celebration of Maundy Thursday has come to mean. Not the foot washing of John's Gospel, but what happened in the upper room during Jesus' last meal with his disciples before his death. He means communion with God and with one another.

We use different words to describe the different aspects of what we commonly call "communion." Those words describe what Jesus means by "love."

Love means "**eucharist.**" Love means "**communion.**" Love means "**supper with the Lord.**"

Love means eucharist. That's an old word meaning "thanksgiving" or "to give thanks." Love requires thanks. Being "lovely" as a congregation means "both giving and accepting thanks." Being loving means being thankful — responding to what God, and those who have been here and gone, and those who sit around us have done for us.

Think about it. You wouldn't be having this time of worship in this way and in this place if it weren't for all the people filling in the blank space around you. You're loved. Are you thankful?

Being loving also means being thankful to God. Somehow in recent generations we've lost that sense of God's providence that says there's something to thank God for. "I take care of me, thank you very much!" Do you really? Is there nothing to be thankful to God for? Self-made people often worship their maker but seldom love their maker. Love requires thanks — to those around us and to the one who made and upholds us.

Love also requires being thanked. It's hard to feel loved when you don't feel appreciated. I don't do nearly enough of it, but do you know what I have consistently gotten the best response from in all the things I do in ministry? A two-line note that says "thank you." Thank you for helping out. Thank you for volunteering. Thank you for giving a little extra. Thank you for your kind words. I can't say I ever thanked anyone for their criticism, but I guess it couldn't hurt!

We gather around this Table every Sunday at first worship and about once-a-month at second worship, and every Maundy Thursday, just as we gather around a family table or a restaurant table every fourth Thursday of November to share bread, drink wine, and give thanks. Love requires it. Feeling loved requires it. Jesus told us to do it. Jesus did it. On this night we call Maundy Thursday, when he shared bread and wine with his disciples for the last time before his death, he took a piece of bread. He gave thanks. He said, "Take it." He took a cup of wine. He gave thanks. He said, "Take it!" Do this. And be thankful.

Do what? Just recollect he was here once? No. Be thankful he's here now with you and me.

Love also means "communion." Commonality. A sense of our oneness; a sharing in our wholeness. In Christ there is no east or west; no south or north. Even Lima is one. That is required for love to be. Loneliness does not make for feeling loved. "Communion" is a ritualized way of expressing togetherness, "community." It tells us we're not alone. We're in it together; and we'd better get it together or we'll never get it — we'll never understand what love means.

In the Scriptures the Hebrew/Jewish people saw their calling as being set apart from the world. In a theological and practical sense they'd moved to the suburbs of life to escape the realities of the cities of life. They were God's people in a Godless world. And they felt pretty smug about it. Guess where Jesus sent them. *"Go,"* (he said) *"and make disciples of all nations..."* (go into that world) *"teaching them to obey everything I have commanded you."*

That's as clear a statement of the oneness of the world community as you'll ever get. And what are we told to go teach? **What he commanded**. Love!

Much as we in this country, like others in other countries, like to assume we have most favored nation status in heaven, what we really have is a question: "What is it love requires of you?" When he was President, George Bush said that love requires of us that we stand down our SAC bombers and destroy our weapons of destruction. One can almost hear Isaiah, the prophet of Israel: *"... they shall beat their swords into plowshares, and their spears into pruning hooks; nation shall not lift up sword against nation, neither shall they learn war any more"* (Isaiah 2:4). Is that so? Yes! When we learn what love requires. A Republican said so! And Jesus said so! (And those, by the way, *are* different!)

I've made no secret of the fact that my greatest frustration with my chosen community is our continuing lack of community and our seeming lack of understanding that it's *required*. That I cannot sit over here, and insist that you stay over there, and find communion and love — which is what "community" is all about. There was a letter in *The Lima News* a while back with the headline: "Wanting Tax Isn't the Same as Needing It." That's the kind of thing we rightly decide at the polls. You can have my opinion on any of that stuff any time you want it. But I can say right up here that "wanting love *is* the same as needing it," and "wanting community *is* the same as needing it." Our town, our neighbors, we ourselves, need a lot of love.

The hymn says,"They'll know we are Christians by our love." Do they know by your love and mine?

I'm reading a book on marriage that has a lot to say about relationships between two people that can be translated for relationships between lots of people. It says that the things that make us angriest out there are really reflections of things "in here." Whatever Lima is, Lima is us! You and me! What does love mean? What would it mean for you and me truly to love this town? Let me suggest that our community requires the same thing our families and our church require. The same thing a communion requires: **the presence of the Lord.**

That's what **"Lord's Supper"** means: supper with the Lord. A Lord who is here. Not just "there" in our common memory, but *here* in our common life. I like to explain Communion for Protestants as being a gathering at the table where the Lord is not *on* the table but *at* the table. The Lord is host. The minister is hired help. If we're here thankfully and together, in Eucharist and Communion, the Lord is here at his supper. He's here with all the love we need, reminding us of all that love requires of you and me.

God loves to lift you and me from hell to heaven. From Good Friday to Easter morn.

Jesus told Judas to go and do what he had to do. Jesus tells you and me to **go love.**

Where, In This Hell, Is The Holy?

John 18:1—19:42

I am convinced that few of us are *really* convinced that this Good Friday really leads to the first day of a *new* week and a new day and a new life. That Good Friday gets us anywhere near an Easter Sunday and what the Psalmist calls "The goodness of the Lord in the land of the living" (Psalm 27:13 *NRSV*).

We call this week "Holy Week." Holy? How so? It was a week of treachery, shallow commitments, following the crowd, betrayal, lying, selling out, broken promises, politics as usual, jealousy, despair, dashed hopes, insecurity, hate, anger, getting even, pain, fear, fraud, fraught with intrigue and murder and the death of an innocent man. Hear anything in that that's holy?

I looked up "Holy Week" in a dozen different references. They all define it this way: It starts with Palm Sunday, and ends with Easter Sunday. In between there's a story that would outdo any afternoon soap opera for twists and turns, but not a word about why it's "holy"! The dictionary says "Holy Week" is the English translation of the Latin, *settimanta santa*, literally "a holy week."

In my research I did discover a new week: "Bright week," a week of brilliant light. That's what our friends the Russian Orthodox call *next* week. But what about *this* week? This "Holy Week"? I can understand calling the week that begins with Easter and resurrection "bright." I find it hard to understand calling the week that begins in the triumph on Palm Sunday and ends in tragedy on Good Friday "holy."

It makes about as much sense as the Palm Sunday hymn:

Ride on! Ride on in majesty!
Hark all the tribes hosanna cry;
O Savior meek, pursue thy road
With palms and scattered garments strowed.

Ride on! Ride on in majesty!
In lowly pomp ride on to die....[1]

As my kids say these days: "*Excuse* me?!" That's a little like saying to someone, "Go to hell; you'll like it!"

That is, in fact, where Jesus was going that first Good Friday — to hell. In the Apostles' Creed there is a phrase, the meaning of which is not entirely clear. In the traditional version it reads: "*... He was crucified, dead and buried.* **He descended into hell.**" I once had a Confirmation Class that recited the creed: "He *ascended* into hell." The creed says that after the resurrection "*he ascended into* **heaven.**" They got their words wrong, but they got the theology right. Because wherever he went after death, Jesus "ascended into hell" when he ascended the cross. He went up into hell by our hands. And it wasn't gold-leafed; it was blood red.

If that sounds a bit extreme, let me recommend a bit of Holy Week reading. First, read from the Bible the story of Holy Week. Try to read it from the perspective of Jesus' friends; people who lived through it not understanding how it would end. Then read from *The Journal of the American Medical Association* an article by William D. Edwards, MD, of the Department of Pathology at the Mayo Clinic. The article is titled "On The Physical Death of Jesus Christ." I'm sure you would not want to read it right now. In a later editorial the *Journal's* editors described Jesus' death as "perhaps the most influential single event of torture in history ..."[2]

One little bit, though. Dr. Edwards writes: "*Jesus of Nazareth underwent Jewish and Roman trials, was flogged, and was sentenced to death by crucifixion. The scourging produced deep stripe like lacerations and appreciable blood loss ... the major pathophysiologic effect of crucifixion was an interference with normal respiration ... death resulted primarily from hypovolemic shock and exhaustion asphyxia. Jesus' death was ensured by the thrust of a soldier's spear into his side.*"[3]

The medical terms are "hypovolemic shock and exhaustion asphyxia." The theological term is "hell." Where, in this hell, is the holy? It's here! The holy has ascended into hell on the cross, and descended into the hell in our lives.

We forget that Palm Sunday is also called "Passion Sunday." The "Passion" is the story of Jesus' suffering and death. It is also the story of God's passionate love for you and me. So passionate that the one who lives forever would die for now for you and me — would go to hell itself for you and me.

Dick Underdahl-Peirce writes in an article called "The Horror and the Holy," that "the French writer" Paul Claudel once said that "Christ did not come to do away with suffering; he did not come to explain it; he came to fill it with his Holy presence. Christ came to take up human suffering, to identify with suffering in his total being. *The horror of Good Friday has been filled with the holy."*[4] Holiness is not niceness. Holiness is the presence of God, even in a week like that one, and even in a week like this one.

In recent weeks a member of our congregation suffered a tragic and untimely loss and I've been given permission to share this with you. At the service for the one who died, a friend gave the memorial homily. In part the friend said: "It was an untimely death. A death that shouldn't have happened to one so full of life. A death that made no sense. So let me tell you about another death (he said) of the time when the Lord God Almighty lost his own boy in a cruel, untimely, senseless death. A death that shouldn't have happened to one so good and fine and full of life. You see? What that cross means is that God has been there weeping long before we got here weeping. The mystery of the Christian gospel is that any pain we feel, God feels. Any tears we shed fall on God's cheeks. Any agonizing emptiness we experience God has experienced, too. The God we love doesn't just pull strings; he feels pain. God not only cares. He bleeds. Knowing that doesn't take away our pain. It just reminds us we have somewhere to go with it — to a God who really does lead us through the valley of the shadow of death. And who, as we go, will even let us be angry at him for allowing this death to occur. Who will let us rail and weep and beat his chest 'til it's all out and then will hold us in love 'til we've found our faith again. The one thing we don't have to be is afraid and without hope, for God's arms are too strong, his heart too loving, his experience too like ours, to abandon us to our grief."

I'll not say who wrote that. I'd like to meet him someday. I will say that the one who wrote those words which capture everything this week is about, who so shared the life of his friend that he could share faith in those words, was like the Jew riding into Jerusalem whose name was Jesus who came to share your life and mine and be our friend. Jesus' purpose was to convince us of the always presence of a holy God in the sometimes hell we call life; to save us from our despair; to raise us from our hell.

Underdahl-Peirce describes, in the midst of a horror, a moment of "holy." He says: "A World War II Navy veteran tells of a voyage across the Atlantic in convoy, when suddenly an enemy submarine rose to the surface and they saw a torpedo launched on its deadly mission toward them. There was no time to change course; all the skipper could do was shout through the loudspeaker, 'Boys, this is it!' But a destroyer nearby also saw what was happening and went full speed ahead in order to intercept the torpedo. The destroyer was blown apart, and every one of the crew lost. The veteran, who'd been on the target ship, said, 'The skipper of that destroyer was my best friend.' "[5]

Jesus on the cross is God being our best friend. Jesus on the cross is God putting himself in front of anything and everything that would torpedo your life. So that in this week and every week, even if it's hell, we might find the holy and say with the apostle Paul, as he wrote to the church in Rome: *I am convinced that neither death, nor life, nor angels, nor rulers, nor things present, nor things to come, nor powers, nor height, nor depth, nor anything else in all creation, will be able to separate us from the love of God in Christ Jesus our Lord* (Romans 8:38-39).

Not even Good Friday.

––––––––––––

1. Henry H. Milman, "Ride On, Ride On In Majesty," *The Presbyterian Hymnal*, no. 90, stanzas 1, 2 (Louisville, Kentucky: Westminster/John Knox Press).

2. Dr. William D. Edwards, et al., *The Journal of the American Medical Association*, June 13, 1986.

3. Dr. William D. Edwards, et al., *The Journal of the American Medical Association*, March 21, 1986, p. 1455.

4. *Presbyterian Survey*, April 1987, p. 18.

5. *Ibid.*

The Lord Is Risen!
He Is Risen Indeed! He Really Is!

John 20:1-18

The Lord is risen!
He is risen indeed!
The Lord is risen!
He is risen indeed!
The Lord is risen!
He is risen indeed!
Indeed he is! Really is! For real!
You know about the only place anybody ever says "indeed" is in church. Let's say it like we really mean it. Like we would say it anyplace else.

I'll say, "The Lord is risen!" You say, **"He really is!"** Let's try that: "The Lord is risen!" **("He really is!")**

That was pretty good. Really. But do we really mean it? Really believe it? Really *want* to believe it?

What if he is? For real!?

And even if he is, what does it matter, really? It's Easter. Does it make any difference to anybody? Really? It's been nearly 2,000 years since that first Easter. Nearly 2,000 times Christians have gathered on an annual basis on the first Sunday after the first full moon after the spring equinox and celebrated the resurrection of Jesus Christ. (Now you know how we determine the date.) But, have 2,000 times made any more difference than the first time?

We Christians don't worship on the Sabbath. In direct contravention of commandment number four which says: "Remember the Sabbath day, and keep it holy," we don't. Sabbath day by our calendar is Saturday. Sabbath day by the Jewish calendar starts Friday at sunset and ends Saturday at sunset. Today is Sunday. By everybody's calendar the FIRST day of the week, not the LAST day of the week. Not the Sabbath. Yet here we are. What happened? Why are we here *today*? And does it make any difference in your life and mine? Really?

We're here today because we Christians gather to worship not on the Sabbath Day but on the Lord's Day. On the day of the resurrection of our Lord.

Every Sunday we celebrate what we call "Easter." Every Sunday is a celebration of the Resurrection of Jesus Christ!

That means we've celebrated Easter Day not just 2,000 times since the first one, but 2,000 times 52 times since the first one. Over 100,000 times since the first Easter we Christians have celebrated Easter, on a day like today, in much the same way: some singing, some praying, some preaching, sometimes some eating. Does it matter? Does it make a difference for you or for me?

Well, that depends. As it depended for Mary Magdalene as she stood crying outside his tomb. As it depended for those friends of Jesus huddled together and hopelessly alone that first Easter evening. It depends on whether it's true. Whether the resurrection of Jesus Christ from the dead is "for real." Whether anything really happened or whether everything was really a hoax.

Logic favors the latter. The more you try to talk yourself into belief in the resurrection, the less you're likely to believe. We think seeing is believing. Mary had trouble seeing through her tears, and those scared disciples couldn't even believe what they could see. Jesus walked into the room (through the wall by one account) and "they were startled and terrified, and thought that they were seeing a ghost" (Luke 24:37 *NRSV*).

Well what would you think? What *do* you think? Does it make a difference in your life?

The resurrection holds out promise of life beyond death. But what about life *before* death? What difference does it make if you get to live life later if living life now isn't worth living? Life later *will* be different. I believe that. Life later *will* be better. I believe that. But the basic belief of Christians since Christ was raised from the dead has been that it makes a difference now. A difference in your life and in mine.

As the hymnwriter put it in my favorite psalm: "I believe I shall see the goodness of the Lord in the land of the living" (Psalm 27: 13 *NRSV*). "The land of the living" is where you and I live.

Our belief in resurrection makes a difference — makes us different people. It takes different kinds of people: frightened people, doubting people, people who have no peace, people who've seen death take someone they love, people who've forgotten the promise of their life, people who say "show me," then can't believe their own eyes, people like you and me, and says, as Jesus said to those huddled, heart-broken, horrified disciples, "Hey, Guys, it's me! For real!"

The great truth of Easter is not the absence of Jesus from the tomb, but the presence of Christ in our lives.

And not as God, our good buddy, but as Christ, our gracious Lord. In a sense Jesus said to them I'm as real as you are. But I'm more real than you are. This is what God really means *you* to be. *Like me.* Like I am now.

Resurrection is not the resuscitation of the old me. It is the re-creation of a *new* me. A me that will still be me. A you that will still be you. But not the same old me, and not the same old you. Thank God!

I believe it was Tom Gillespie, the President of Princeton Theological Seminary, who once noted that we are called by God, but that God's call is to more than more of the same. It is a call to newness of life, resurrected life, eternal life, life worth living.

We tend to think of eternal life in terms of our longevity. The Bible thinks of it more in terms of God's creativity. God's creating life anew. Life that is for now, as well as for later.

If you find that hard to believe you're not alone. Jesus' disciples had their doubts. According to the story as Luke's version of the story tells us, on the Sunday following Jesus' death on Friday several women (not just Mary Magdalene) went to the cemetery, found an open grave, and rushed back to town to announce what they'd found — or, rather, what they *had not* found — to Jesus' closest friends.

They didn't believe it. If they dismissed the story, sitting half-a-mile and half-an-hour from the grave, and only two days from his death, how much harder is it for you and me sitting half-a-world and half-of-recorded-history from it!? If you feel alone in your doubts, you ought to try to stand up here when everyone is assuming you don't have any doubts! And even if you do, you're paid not to!

I have a poster in my office with a copy of the classic picture of Jesus praying at Gethsemane and the superscription: *Considering the fact that Jesus had his doubts, why can't you?* Well, I can. And I do. Just like you. Just like those disciples, who even when they saw him doubted it really was him!

John says, "When the disciples saw the Lord they become very happy" (John 20:20 *CEV*).

Luke says, "... in their joy they were disbelieving and still wondering ..." (Luke 24:41 *NRSV*).

"... they stood there undecided, filled with joy and doubt" (*Ibid, The Living Bible,* paraphrase).

"The disciples were so glad and amazed that they could not believe it." (*Ibid, CEV*).

I think Luke comes closest to the truth.

Really now! Can you or I believe it? I think we can. And I believe it makes a difference. All the difference in the world. It's the difference between the living death of so many people's lives, and life forever with our Lord, who said, because I live, you will live also. You *can* live also. And always. Even now.

I just came back from Louisville and a conference with Frank Harrington of the Peachtree Presbyterian Church in Atlanta. Frank talked about living life in a rut. He said a rut is just a grave with the ends knocked out.

Well, eternal life is just living like life starts in the rut where I'm lying, but opens out into life forever, in both directions. Through death there is life forever. And in living as Jesus taught, there is life now.

Life that, as it was for Jesus, is as real as that Sunday dinner you're heading off to shortly. And as real as Luke's account of Jesus' request for something to eat. Their serving him a piece of broiled fish is not just a passing culinary comment. It's confirmation.

He's alive. Dead people don't eat. He's as alive as you and I are right now. And as alive as you and I will be someday.

We Christians are not set as guards at an empty tomb. Trying to make death secure. We are called to witness to a living Lord. To try to make life worth living for us all. Jesus said so. He said to his disciples, "You are witnesses of these things" (Luke 24:48 *NRSV*).

So are we!

The Lord is Risen!

He is risen indeed!

He really is!

The Last Beatitude

John 20:19-31

What the disciples of Jesus reported to their fellow disciple Thomas they had seen seemed unbelievable. And Thomas didn't believe it! They said they saw Jesus alive. Well, Thomas saw him alive until late the previous Friday afternoon when Thomas saw him dead. It was now Sunday afternoon — and to what they said they saw, Thomas' response was, "Seeing is believing," and until I see something different from what I have already seen, I will not believe a word of what you say.

And for that little exchange, Thomas has gone down in history, not as the disciple Thomas, but as "doubting Thomas" — with his own entry in the dictionary! I looked it up. In the dictionary in the church library, a "doubting Thomas" is defined as "a person who refuses to believe without proof; (a) skeptic."[1]

And not just about Jesus. About anything. A "doubting Thomas" is one who when presented with an assertion of fact, asserts his or her right to raise questions, and demand proof, and doesn't believe it until they get it.

Thomas wanted tangible, touchable proof of Jesus' resurrection. He had such proof of Jesus' death. He was there. He wanted the same proof of the claim that Jesus, whom he had seen die, had been seen alive by the other disciples. For Thomas there was no doubt that Jesus was dead, and every reason to doubt that Jesus was alive.

Yet, for his honesty, he has gone down in history as "doubting Thomas" — the man who doubted the resurrection of Jesus Christ. And the term "doubting Thomas" has negative connotations to this day.

But it shouldn't. Because Thomas wasn't and *isn't* alone, even in this room. And Jesus said not one negative word about him. As *Newsweek* magazine reported recently: "From the very beginning, the resurrection of Jesus was met by doubt and disbelief. To the Jews of Biblical Jerusalem, it was simply blasphemous for the renegade Christians to claim that a crucified criminal was the Messiah. To the cultivated Greeks, who believed in the soul's immortality, the very idea of a resurrected body was repugnant. Even among Gnostic Christians of the second century, the preferred view was that Jesus was an immortal spirit who merely discarded his mortal cloak. And yet, if the New Testament is to be believed, it was the appearance of the resurrected Christ that lit the flame of Christian faith, and the power of the Holy Spirit that fired a motley band of fearful disciples to proclaim the Risen Jesus throughout the Greco-Roman world. According to the late German Marxist philosopher, Ernst Bloch (says *Newsweek*), 'It wasn't the morality of the Sermon on the Mount which enabled Christianity to conquer Roman paganism, but the belief that Jesus had been raised from the dead.' "[2]

There you have it, from *Newsweek*, just two weeks ago — never mind 2,000 years ago. The bottomline is what Thomas refused to believe — couldn't believe — without proof: that "the Lord is risen"; that "Christ the Lord Is Risen Today"; that "Jesus Christ Is Risen Today." [3] We say it. We sing it. Do we sincerely believe it? Or down deep do we, like Thomas, tend to doubt it?

Don't answer that. It's the wrong question. Nothing in the text says that Thomas *doubted* anything. Nor does it say we shouldn't. I know that the story I read has Jesus saying: "Do not doubt, but believe" (John 20:27 *NRSV*). But that isn't the literal translation of Jesus' words to Thomas. It is only one possible interpretation historically conditioned by hindsight about what Thomas had to confront. In the Greek text Jesus says to Thomas, "Do not be unbelieving but believing." Thomas would be better called "Unbelieving Thomas" or "Thomas who couldn't believe the unbelievable just because someone told him to."

Whichever, put that way, Jesus' intent is not just that Thomas stop his "doubting," his questioning, his thinking, the use of "the little grey cells," but that he start believing. The one has to do with debating the facts; the other with putting our trust in something or someone. The one involves my intellect; the other my whole life. The one involves my accepting something as true; the other my discovery that I am accepted by the one who calls himself "the truth" (John 14:6 *NRSV*).

It is not now and never has been, when it comes to the resurrection of Jesus Christ, a matter of "proving it," so much as "believing in it." And believing in what it means for you and me. That, as we have just sung, "From death to life eternal, From this world to the sky, Our Christ hath brought us over, with hymns of victory." [4]

Read the *Newsweek* article to which I've already alluded, or the similar *Time* magazine article published the same week. Both were cover stories for Easter. *Time*'s cover read, "The Search for Jesus," and goes on, "Some scholars are debunking the Gospels. Now traditionalists are fighting back. What are Christians to believe?"[5]

According to the self-appointed "Jesus Seminar" reported on in the article, the answer is "very little." According to them, "Jesus, in fact, 'is an imaginative theological construct, into which have been woven traces of that enigmatic sage from Nazareth — traces that cry out for recognition and liberation from the firm grip of those whose faith overpowered their memories.' "[6]

Members of the so-called Jesus Seminar are doing no more than Thomas did, in a sense. Demanding proof. But belief demands more. As Baptist minister Craig Blomberg puts it in the *Time* article: "You could say ... belief builds on the direction the evidence is already pointing."[7] You can prove things to a point, but beyond that point comes belief. Comes trust in the one to whom the evidence is pointing.

That was certainly true for Thomas. With the evidence literally at hand, he did not simply say, "He is risen indeed!" but rather, he said, "My Lord and my God!" (John 20:28 *NRSV*).

That's more than a simple, "Gee, guys, you're right! He's alive."

That's a statement of belief far beyond simply not doubting what the other disciples had said. "My Lord and my God" is a faith statement of the first order. A belief statement far beyond bickering over biblical facts.

The United Bible Societies' handbook on John's Gospel, written to aid those who translate the Bible into other languages, may be helpful in this regard. It says of Thomas' words, "My Lord and my God": "In certain languages one cannot possess such terms as 'Lord' or 'God.' If so, it may be necessary to translate 'you are the one who rules over me, and you are the one whom I worship.' " [8] That's what Thomas meant.

In the Greek text of our New Testament Thomas calls Jesus "The Lord of me and the God of me."[9] My Lord! My God! I believe! That's more than Thomas could have come up with on his own. More than anyone was asking him to believe. And certainly more than the evidence could "prove." Even a dead man walking could only point in that direction.

What Jesus says next is sometimes taken as a putdown of Thomas and those who have a need to "see" — those whose faith goes seeking things that are provably true: Well, so what, Thomas! What you had to see to believe, others will believe without seeing. Blessed are the others!

But that's the wrong reading. Thomas' blessing was no less because he saw and believed. Raymond Brown translates, "You have believed because you have seen me, (Thomas). Happy are those who have not seen and yet have believed."[10]

It's not a negative statement: "You had to see to believe, Thomas ... Better believing is not seeing ..." But a simple statement: "Thomas, you, like the other disciples, have the privilege of seeing and believing ... Others will not see — but will still believe — blessed are those also!"

Those — who? Who is Jesus talking about in this last "beatitude" — this final "blessed"? Those still to come. Those like you and me. We are those Jesus calls blessed in our struggle to believe. Those who cannot "see," but somehow come to believe, as best we can, in Jesus Christ.

So what do you believe when it comes right down to it? An awful lot of us, I find, believe that God doesn't like us. He puts us down — as we think Jesus did to Thomas. We know we're supposed to believe that he loves us, but we've never been sure he really likes us. And we're never quite sure what he might do as a result.

Much of Christianity has confused the situation further by making Christian belief into an entrance exam for the hereafter. As though having the right answers, at the right time, will get you into the right place, or out of the wrong one. That in turn has led to dividing ourselves between what I'm supposed to believe and what I really believe. What I'm supposed to believe counts later. I'll get around to that later. What I really believe counts now. I'll get around to that much sooner.

But belief for the writer of John's Gospel, belief for Jesus, was more than that. It *is* more than that. Belief is more than just ascertaining the facts and figures of faith. Or figuring out the best way to keep God happy long enough to get me into heaven. Belief is living life now certain of the love of God in Jesus Christ for you and me. Living life unafraid — even of death itself.

That's good news. Something in which to believe in a bad news world, in a world that needs some good news. There is a God who, when we are at our worst, still calls forth our best through our belief in his love. Says the hymn: "Love drowned in death will never die."[11] Such love God has shown in the life, death, and resurrection of Jesus Christ.

Trouble is even we, like Thomas, sometimes don't see it and hesitate to believe it. And sometimes it seems to come out that the "good news" about God, is really the "bad news" about us. Repent, we say, and God will forgive you. And some, with television time to fill up and pay for, say it over and over and over, assuring all of us that none of us has ever repented quite enough to please God (or pay their media bills). The problem becomes then: How do we do that if we believe that? How do we ever get to the point of "getting it" — like Thomas?

Well, of course God forgives those who repent. God forgives and forgets all that stuff you and I can't seem to forgive or forget.

But the Good News is better than that! We may doubt it, but it's true. The Good News is God doesn't need our permission to love us and save us. And he doesn't ask for it before he does it. As the poet puts it:

I sought the Lord,
and afterward I knew
he moved my soul to seek him,
seeking me;
It was not I that found,
O Savior true —
No,
I was found
by·thee.[12]

What Thomas could finally see, was something we can still
see, something we can believe in. That, as the hymn we'll sing
shortly puts it:

Christ is alive, and comes to bring
Good news to this and every age,
'Til earth and sky and ocean ring
With joy, with justice, love, and praise.[13]

To the living one, *our* Lord and *our* God, Jesus Christ.

(For Further Reading: "The Jesus Seminar's misguided quest for
the historical Jesus," *Christian Century*, January 3-10, 1996.)

1. *The Random House Dictionary of the English Language.*

2. *Newsweek*, April 8, 1996.

3. Hymn titles found in *The Presbyterian Hymnal*, no. 113 and no. 112 (Louisville, Kentucky: Westminster/John Knox Press).

4. "The Day Of Resurrection," *The Presbyterian Hymnal*, no. 118 (Louisville,
Kentucky: Westminster/John Knox Press).

5. *Time*, April 8, 1996, cover.

6. *Ibid.*, p. 54.

7. *Ibid.*, p. 59.

8. Barclay M. Newman and Eugene A. Nida, *A Handbook on The Gospel of John*, UBS Handbook Series, (New York: United Bible Societies, 1980), p. 619.

9. *The Zondervan Parallel New Testament in Greek and English* (Grand Rapids, Michigan: Zondervan Bible Publishers, 1980), p. 339.

10. Raymond M. Brown, *The Gospel According to John XIII-XXI: A New Translation with Introduction and Commentary* (Garden City, New York: Doubleday & Company, Inc., 1978), p. 1019.

11. Brian Wry, "Christ Is Alive!" *The Presbyterian Hymnal*, no. 108 (Louisville, Kentucky: Westminster/John Knox Press).

12. Source unknown.

13. Brian Wry, "Christ Is Alive!" *The Presbyterian Hymnal*, no. 108 (Louisville, Kentucky: Westminster/John Knox Press).

People Die!

Luke 24:13-35

"**People** die. Don't ya know." That's what Cleopas and his friend said to Jesus on Easter afternoon on their way home. People die!

Don't believe it? Don't want to believe it? Read about it in *The Lima News*. And not just in the obits. This is my copy of *The Lima News* from Good Friday, the day we remember that Jesus died.

Page 1: Cult Died in Shifts

Page 2: A headline so gruesome, let's just say, "Wife kills husband."

Page 3: A list of the dead from page 1, by age, sex, and the state where they got their driver's license.

Page 4: A story about the continuing and never-ending O J murder case.

Page 5: A story about serial killer Charles Manson.

Page 6: An editorial about air-bags, designed to save lives, now known possibly to cause deaths.

Page 7: More on the mass suicide in California:

> *QUOTE: "For them, death was not tragic. For people who called themselves monks and lived in a virtual computer cloister, tied to each other and to astrological portents, death was apparently not an end as much as a transition. 'I'm sure they were convinced of their immortality,' said Dr. James Breckenridge, professor of religion at Baylor University in Waco, Texas."* [1]

To believe that you're immortal is to believe that you are not mortal, that you not only will not, but that you *cannot* die. Thirty-nine people died last week believing that. They proved only that people die, like Cleopas and his friend said that first Easter day.

By the time I got through all that it was a relief finally to get to famous-maker sunglasses at 25 percent off and Saville Row sport-coats at 35 percent off at the after-Easter sales.

A lot of people's minds, (like a lot of our minds?) are closed when it comes to the meaning of Easter. People think it is a holy day that seems to mean that people do not die. But then they do. We've mixed the message. **The message of Easter is that Jesus lives, not that people don't die.**

And people who do die are not in a holding pattern over some heavenly heliport, and they do not find their hope in something hiding behind the Hale Bopp comet.

Death is not a boarding pass for life. And Christianity is not about denying death. It's about the defeat of death in resurrection, in restoration to life by God through Jesus Christ — a defeat that does not deny the reality of death, but says we can live with that reality in assurance that God really raises those who do die to life forever with him.

It's not that I don't die, but that I do live, and that I can live now, life now, and a resurrected life someday like that of Jesus Christ.

More comforting, I think, than the notion that Grandma lives on somewhere, is the belief that Grandma will live forever some-day, not in the worn-out body where she spent her last days, but in a resurrected body, a recreated body, where she will spend eternal days with Christ.

As the creed we will say says, "I believe in the resurrection of the body and the life everlasting." That's the meaning of Easter.

The meaning of Holy Week is that Jesus died. "(He) suffered under Pontius Pilate, was crucified, *died*, and was buried. He de-scended to the dead."

He was dead, dead as a doornail, which my dictionary defines as "undoubtedly dead."[2]

There are a lot of dead doornails in here. No, I don't mean you! I counted them. There are precisely 2,128 symbols of just how dead Jesus was nailed into the doors at the back of the sanctuary where most of you came in this morning. Doornails are nails in doors used to strengthen and decorate them. There are 2,128 doornails nailed in the doors to this room. And at last count, they're all dead. They didn't die. They were never alive. But we are. Jesus was. And dead as a doornail he was and we shall be.

If you find that disconcerting, you are not alone. The denial of death is something we humans have been doing as long as we've been alive. The early church had to deal with an early heresy called "gnosticism." The gnostics, much like the cult in California, thought they knew something the rest of us didn't — that people who die, really don't.

It's amazing how much theology you get in newspapers and magazines these days. One of *The Lima News* articles quotes William Dinges, who teaches about new religions at Catholic University in Washington, D.C. Says Dinges, "They very well might have lived as computer age 'gnostics,' initiates of a select group, with access to special, arcane truths.

"Part of the mystique of the ancient tradition of gnosticism is that it is 'very antimaterialistic,' said Dinges. 'If you see your body as a prison and matter as bad, it's 'I'm outta here.' "[3]

Even on the next UFO out of town!

Such beliefs deny the goodness of what God has made. And the church since the beginning has condemned such beliefs as meaningless madness. As meaningless and as mad as the death of 39 young, bright, apparently well-to-do men and women, who in checking out of earthly life thought they were only checking in to life beyond the stars.

The church has long rejected the notion that like the cult in California we should put our hope in death as a transition to life, instead of in the God of life who defeats death in Jesus Christ.

Death is the end, says the church. But that end portends God's creating a new beginning. Christian hope is in the resurrection of the body, a new body — not the old one — a new life, a God-given life, for you, for me, in Jesus Christ. A life that I am to claim not by claiming that ending this life will make my life better, but by living this life as it is, and making of it all that it can be, in anticipation of life as it will be, beyond death. Death that will come to me as surely as it came to Jesus himself.

Dead as the nails in those doors, he was. Yet Jesus is now as alive as everyone in this room, and because he lives we shall live also.

I recently saw a sign outside a church that said, "The empty tomb is the foundation of our faith." I know what they're saying. But they're saying it wrongly. "The Church's *one foundation* is Jesus Christ her Lord." Her living Lord. Our Lord. Who is alive! And who calls you and me to live like we believe it.

There are lots of reasons not to believe it. Just read your newspaper! Cleopas and friend didn't believe it, even when they were looking right at it.

In the story I read from Luke the two followers of Jesus are heading home because what they had hoped for, and dreamed of, had died. There was no point in hanging around. On Friday he was hanging on a cross. Then they hauled him down and put him in a hole in the ground. Some silly women said they saw him alive. But the first stage of facing death is to deny it. If it's too good to be true, it is. Too bad. That's life! That's right, said Jesus, as "he interpreted to them the things about himself in all the scriptures" (Luke 24:27 *NRSV*). Scriptures that never deny death. But Scriptures that also always hold out hope of life.

But with life staring them right in the face, Cleopas and his companion didn't believe it. Lots of commentators have wondered why. Maybe Jesus wore a hood. Or they were blinded by their tears. Or they were in shock. You could even say, they were taking Jesus' death very well. They weren't denying it. On their way home, they were on their way to dealing with the death of their friend in a psychologically healthy way, we would say.

All of which may have been true. But the simple truth for me is simply that if someone I loved and cared about died, and then showed up two days after the funeral, I doubt I'd see it either. I know I wouldn't. And if I thought I did, I'd deny it.

We have a capacity for what psychologists call "cognitive dissonance." Jesus died. Dead people don't live. Jesus is dead. If you see him alive, "cognitive dissonance" takes care of it. We bring what we experience into line with what we know. And that's what we believe. That's how we survive, psychologically, in this confusing world. These two men, or maybe it was a man and a woman, were survivors. Jesus wasn't. He died, don't you know!?

Well, he did. But he rose again from the dead. And those two people, like people ever since, found him "... made known to them in the breaking of the bread" (Luke 24:35 *NRSV*).

That bread on the Table. It's there to tell us one thing.

The Lord is Risen!

He is Risen Indeed!

And as he was with Cleopas and friend, he's here breaking bread with you and me.

---

1. *The Lima News*, 3/28/97.

2. *The Random House Dictionary of the English Language.*

3. *The Lima News*, 3/28/97.

Why Sheep?

John 10:1-10

Why sheep?

Today is sometimes called "Sheep Sunday" by preachers, because this Sunday every year the lessons are like the lessons this morning, John's description of Jesus, the Good Shepherd, and the Psalmist's song, "The Lord Is My Shepherd." So, I wondered aloud to myself, as I read these words, why **sheep**?

Why not eagles? Why not think of you and me as eagles in a gorgeous blue sky, instead of sheep in some muddy pasture. Isaiah writes ... "They who wait for the Lord shall renew their strength. They shall mount up with wings like eagles, they shall run and not be weary, they shall walk and not faint" (Isaiah 40:31). That sounds good — that's why I have a plaque with those words on my office wall. Why not call you and me eagles? **Why sheep!?**

Then I got honest, and thought maybe it's because the prayer of confession got it right: "... we *have* erred and strayed from God's ways like lost sheep. We *have* followed too much the devices and desires of our own hearts ..." and so forth and so on.

We seldom soar, like eagles; we often act like sheep. As the song puts it:

> *We are poor little lambs who have lost our way,*
> *Baa! Baa! Baa!*
> *We're little black sheep who've gone astray,*
> *Baa! Baa! Baa!*
> *Gentlemen-rankers out on the spree,*
> *   damned from here to eternity,*

God ha' mercy on such as we,
Baa! Baa! Baa!

Some of us are old enough to remember that as the "Whiffenpoof Song," popularized in the '30s and '40s by the singer Rudy Vallee. It was originally part of a poem by Rudyard Kipling. And I thought it would make a great prayer of confession, if we could sing it or say it with a straight face.

Let's try it. Repeat after me:

We're poor little lambs who've lost our way ...
We're little black sheep who've gone astray ...
God have mercy on such as we! ...
Baaaa! Baaaa! Baaaaa!

But whatever our words, our confession is still only a refrain to our lives, as Kipling's words are only the refrain to his poem. Kipling's poem reads, in part, like too many lives:

We have done with Hope and Honour,
*   we are lost to Love and Truth,*
We are dropping down the ladder rung by rung,
And the measure of our torment
*   is the measure of our youth.*
*   God help us, for we knew the worst too young!*
Our shame is clean repentance
*   for the crime that brought the sentence,*
*   Our pride it is to know no spur of pride,*

And the Curse of Reuben holds us
*   till an alien turf enfolds us*
And we die, and none can tell Them where we died.
We're poor little lambs who've lost our way,
*   Baa! Baa! Baa!*[1]

We have erred *and* strayed — like lost sheep. I know that. You know that. The Bible knows that, and uses that as a metaphor for the reality of our lives. Lives we live together in our families, at our work, in our community, in this church every day.

And it's our life lived together that the Frugal Gourmet, Jeff Smith, sees explaining why the biblical metaphor for you and me is "sheep." His latest book serves up some wonderful sounding recipes for lamb chops, grilled, with mint and cinnamon, in grape leaves; and lamb stew with figs and wine. He says the sheep metaphor finds its meaning in the fact that "sheep are communal by their very nature. (Pointing out that) As a matter of fact we do not even have a word for one sheep. The term is always understood to be plural."[2]

I'm skeptical of anyone who writes of the love of God for his "sheep," and how to cook lambchops, in the same book. But maybe the Frugal Gourmet, who happens to be a Methodist minister, as well as a good cook, is right. The meaning of the metaphor is simply that you and I *together*, like sheep — plural — are a community, a flock of faith in which we are cared for by God as a shepherd cares for sheep, and that's what God intends. We're in it together, and together we are shepherded by Jesus Christ.

That's a good corrective to the excessive individualism of our day that leaves so many of us feeling very much alone in the presence of almighty God. More like a sheep at the mercy of a predator, than a lamb in God's arms of protection. Protection provided in Jesus' story by the sheep being together in the sheepfold — not just in his willingness to run around willy-nilly to find them.

The nineteenth century Princeton theologian, Benjamin Breckinridge Warfield, whose work was to have great influence in our century on the original "Fundamentalists," apparently considered this to be fundamental: "That in Jesus Christ, God was 'saving the world and not merely one individual here and there out of the world.'"[3] That in Jesus Christ God came as a shepherd, to his sheep.

The children's poem says, Mary had *a* "little lamb." And the classic picture of Jesus, the good shepherd, has him carrying *a* single lamb on his shoulders. But the biblical picture has him surrounded by an uncountable herd of sheep. To paraphrase the children's book by Wanda Gag, there are sheep here, sheep there, sheep and little lambs everywhere; hundreds of sheep, thousands of sheep, millions and billions and trillions of sheep. All being sheep and all in need of a shepherd.

So Charles Cousar writes, "The language (in John's gospel) is reminiscent of the Twenty-third Psalm. What is eloquently sung there about the Lord's care, guidance, and protection of the flock is here (in John) reaffirmed in terms of Jesus."[4]

It's that in-it-togetherness that John Wurster was talking about last week, when he said, "... sure, it's possible to encounter Christ anywhere, but the biblical witness is that that encounter is most likely to happen in a place where people are gathered ..." (John Wurster, 4/21/96). He said to worship and break bread. I'll say to be shepherded by the one who calls himself the Good Shepherd. People gathered, like sheep in a sheepfold, are those most likely to encounter the shepherd. People gathered like sheep in a sheepfold can be shepherded — brought together in warmth, and the safety of life together. Yes, the Good Shepherd goes after one lost sheep — but why? — to return him to the fold, to the flock.

I did a little research. This book called *Approved Practices in Sheep Production* says that in caring for sheep, "Most important is that ... continuous attention (is) required. Sheep are often quite helpless and fall easy prey to predators, especially dogs, coyotes, foxes, bobcats, and eagles. They might even fall prey to such hazards as picket or woven wire fences, or to ditches and gullies in which they might lie and suffocate unless aid came quickly. Parasites and disease are also ever present problems to guard against."[5]

The book says sheep have a lot of problems. So do we. The book says sheep face a lot of dangers. So do we. The book says sheep are best tended together. So are we, says the book we call the Bible with its image of God as our shepherd.

But what about me? Well, what about me? The image of the sheepfold and you and me as the sheep is not intended to make us feel sheepish, or to make us feel individually unimportant; rather it is intended to reinforce the importance of all of us to the shepherd who is God in Jesus Christ. The sheepfold, then, while constraining and confining and sometimes crowded is not claustrophobic. Rather, by setting limits on how far we can stray, and what can get at us, it frees us to live life as God intends: to live each day to the fullest — what Jesus meant when he said, "I came that they might have life, and have it abundantly" (John 10:10 *NRSV*). "I came so that everyone would have life, and have it in its fullest" (John 10:10 CEV).

Some of the fullest moments in my ministry have been moments filled by many of you. I had such a moment recently when someone shared a poem with me that has meant much to them in their life. It's called "Live Each Day to the Fullest," and describes what life lived that way — what Jesus called abundant life — might look like. I asked and they said I could share it with you. It goes:

> *LIVE* *each day to the fullest*
> *GET* *the most from each hour, each day, and each age of your life.*
> *Then you can look forward with confidence and back without regrets.*
> *BE* *yourself — but be your best self.*
> *DARE* *to be different and to follow your own star.*
> *And don't be afraid to be happy.*
> *ENJOY* *what is beautiful.*
> *LOVE* *with all your heart and soul.*
> *BELIEVE* *that those you love, love you.*
> *LEARN* *to forgive yourself for your faults,*
>   *for this is the first step in learning to forgive others.*
> *LISTEN* *to those whom the world may consider uninteresting,*
>   *for each person has, in himself, something of worth.*
>
> *DISREGARD* *what the world owes you,*
>   *and concentrate on what you owe the world.*
> *FORGET* *what you have done for your friends,*
>   *and remember what they have done for you.*
> *No matter how troublesome the cares of life*
>   *may seem to you at times,*
>   *this is still a beautiful world —*
> *And you are at home in it,*
>   *as a child is at home in his parents' house.*
> *When you are faced with a decision,*
> *MAKE* *that decision as wisely as possible —*
>   *then forget it.*

The moment of absolute certainty never arrives;
*... **ACT** as if everything depended upon you, and*
***PRAY** as if everything depended upon God.*
— S. H. Payer

If you live like that, if I live like that, if we live like that to-gether, **and even when we don't** live like that, or think we can't live like that, we *can* depend upon God, the good shepherd, whom we know in Jesus Christ, our shepherd, who is well described in the shepherd David's most famous Psalm.

We've had a new Apostles' Creed, and a new Lord's Prayer. A new Twenty-third Psalm will complete the set. Listen:

You, LORD, are my shepherd.
I will never be in need.
You let me rest in fields of green grass.
You lead me to streams of peaceful water,
and you refresh my life.

You are true to your name,
and you lead me along the right paths.
I may walk through valleys as dark as death,
but I won't be afraid.
You are with me,
and your shepherd's rod makes me feel safe.
You treat me to a feast,
while my enemies watch.
You honor me as your guest,
and you fill my cup until it overflows.
Your kindness and love will always be with me
each day of my life,
and I will live forever in your house, LORD.
— Psalm 23 *(CEV)*

Without fail, when someone has died someone will say, "Please read that." What the Bible says is *live* that — every day! In this world where the closest most of us ever get to a sheep is a book or the wool in our suit, our skirt, our slacks, or our socks, we still need a shepherd — to lead us and guide us and occasionally prod us in the way we should go. And the good shepherd, who gives his life for the life of the sheep, for your life and mine, that we might live and have life abundantly, is Jesus Christ.

---

1. "Gentlemen Rankers" by Rudyard Kipling.

2. Jeff Smith, *The Frugal Gourmet Keeps the Feast: Past, Present, and Future* (William Morrow & Company, November 1, 1995), p. 20.

3. Bradley J. Longfield, *The Presbyterian Controversy: Fundamentalists, Modernists and Moderates (Religion in America)* (Oxford University Press, November 1, 1993), p. 45.

4. W. Brueggemann, et al., *Texts for Preaching, A Lectionary Commentary Based on the NRSV — Year A* (Louisville, Kentucky: Westminster/John Knox Press, 1995), p. 290.

5. Elwood M. Juergenson, *Approved Practices in Sheep Production* (Danville, Illinois: Interstate Printers & Publishers, 1981), p. 6.

This Is Certain

John 14:1-14

J_{ESUS} said, **"Do not let your hearts be troubled. Believe in God, believe also in me"** (John 14:1 *NRSV*).

Since everything that follows for the rest of the passage I just read from John is commentary on that, we need to hear that clearly, before we hear anything else.

This is the closest English can get to the Greek of John's Gospel: "Let not be troubled of you the heart; Believe in God, also in me believe."[1]

And here are the translations of others who have listened and interpreted these words for you and me:

"Let your hearts not be disturbed. Believe in God and believe in me" (Lattimore).

"Don't be worried! Have faith in God and have faith in me" (*CEV*).

"Do not let your hearts be troubled. Trust in God still, and trust in me" (*Jerusalem Bible*).

"Set your troubled hearts at rest. Trust in God always; trust also in me" (*New English*).

"You must not let yourselves be distressed — you must hold on to your faith in God and to your faith in me" (*Phillips*).

" 'Do not be worried and upset,' Jesus told them. 'Believe in God and believe also in me' " (*TEV*).

"Do not let your hearts be troubled. You have faith in God; have faith, then, in me" (*The Anchor Bible*).

What follows in the text has Jesus saying to us, have faith, trust, in face of **uncertainty about death**, **uncertainty about life**, and

uncertainty about whether anything is to be done about either one of them anyway. This isn't a three-point sermon, really. It's three sermons, with one point. As Jesus puts it a little later, "**Do not let your hearts be troubled, and do not let them be afraid**" (John 14:27 *NRSV*).

In face of death, there is a future for you — it's with me, said Jesus. In face of life, there's a way for you — it's with me, said Jesus. In face of uncertainty about whether it's worth trying at all, you have my promise. "If in my name you ask me for anything, I will do it," said Jesus (John 14:14 *NRSV*).

Die unafraid. Live unafraid. Ask unafraid. That's it!

I'm summarizing up front this morning, so if anybody fades out halfway through, you can still get it. That's it. What God wants for you and for me is for us to quit being fearful people and for us to start being faithful people — a faithful person being not just one who believes a lot of doctrine about God, but rather one whose trust is in God in the uncertainties of life and death.

Believing, as we Presbyterians put it in our *Brief Statement of Faith*, "That in life and death we belong to God ... (and) with believers in every time and place, we rejoice that nothing in life or in death can separate us from the love of God in Christ Jesus our Lord."

Nothing! But in spite of that affirmation, drawn from the apostle Paul, we've all got a list of things we think might separate us (or others) from God's love. Clarence Macartney catalogued some of our problems in a Memorial Day address a while back: "Widespread murder, rampant divorce, the decline of family religion, rising hemlines, blatant hedonism, and apostate preachers all ... (signal) a seriously diseased society."[2]

He's right — pretty much. As right now as he was on Memorial Day, 1927! There's a lot about the way we live and the way we die that would lead one to wonder whether there is any hope for you and me, here or hereafter, which makes us uncertain about both. But when our wondering hearts become worrying hearts, Jesus says, "Don't worry. God is still God. I am still with you. Do not be afraid." He didn't say, "Don't be concerned." He didn't say, "Don't try to do anything about it." On the contrary, he said, "Do something about your concerns without fear. I am with you all the way!"

Three points about what that means.

1. In death, there is a place for you.
2. In life, there is a way for you.
3. In uncertainty, we'll find our way together.

In death, there is a place for you and me. If it will help you remember, attach this point to the popular song, "There's a place for us," from *West Side Story*. I don't remember where the place was in the song, but in death your place and my place is with Jesus Christ. Jesus said so. There is a place for us in the kingdom of God.

In the *King James Version* of the Bible, the place is called a "mansion." "In my Father's house are many mansions ..." said Jesus (John 14:2 *KJV*). As a child growing up, I tried to imagine what that would look like. I knew what a "mansion" looked like. Down South a "mansion" looked like Tara in the movie *Gone With the Wind*. My problem was how you got a bunch of Taras — a bunch of antebellum mansions — in a house. Newer translations solved that problem. "Mansions" became "dwelling places" or "rooms."

The United Bible Society handbook on John, used by biblical translators, says, "*My Father's house* is best taken as a phrase descriptive of heaven as a place having *many rooms* (that is, room enough for all)."[3]

I still like to think in terms of "mansions," but a mansion can be a fairly exclusive place. Jesus clearly intends that there is room in his "mansion" for us all.

When death is what scares you, be that the death of someone you love, the death of hopes and dreams, the death of some fondly-held belief, or the death that comes to everyone who lives, even you, find your security in me, says Jesus. In death there is a place for you with me.

But as "Dr. Death," Dr. Jack Kervorkian, all too uneasily reminds us, for some of us there is something worse than death. It's called life. Jesus said, **"In life there is a way for you."** There is a way to live that's worth living. Not just what Kervorkian offers — or what drugs or alcohol offer — a way out. But what Jesus offers — a way through life and into life worth living forever. Not only is there a *place* for you at the end of life, there is a *way* for you in life.

And "I am the way, and the truth, and the life," said Jesus (John 14:6 *NRSV*). That could sound a bit arrogant, unless you understand that what is being offered is the truth about life and a way to live it. The truth is, life is worth living. It's worth living well. And Jesus' way is the way to do that.

Too often these words, coupled with Jesus' words, "No one comes to the Father except through me" (John 14:6 *NRSV*), have been misused by some to say, "No one comes to the Father except us...." There is only a "place" for those who believe as we do, who walk the way we walk. Sometimes that's a misguided attempt to take Jesus at his word. Other times it's a blatant attempt to have the last word for ourselves. We know the way, and others better get with it, or God will get'em! That way is not the way of the God we know in Jesus Christ.

Jesus said, "Whoever has seen me has seen the Father" (John 14:9 *NRSV*). That's a clear warning not to misunderstand God's relationship to you and me as some kind of "good cop/bad cop" game, with Jesus as the "good cop," reassuring us God loves us, and God as the "bad cop" threatening us if we don't love him. It's one thing to say, "If you want to see God, look at Jesus." It's quite another to say, "Go to hell, if you don't see it."

And that is not the way of Jesus Christ. The way Jesus summed up elsewhere in response to those who asked him what was most important about the way we live. He didn't say it is most important to figure out for ourselves who's right and who's wrong, but simply to live together Jesus' way: "... love the Lord your God with all your heart, and with all your soul, and with all your mind, and with all your strength, (and) ... love your neighbor as yourself" (Mark 12:30-31 *NRSV*).

There is a lot we *can* do, but there is very little we *should* do before we do that: before we love God, love our neighbor and, in doing that, discover we can love ourselves.

Someone once said that contrary to what would seem to be true, Christianity has not failed as a way to live. It's simply that so few have ever tried it. Whatever else the passage may connote, some kindness and love "along the way" are clearly what Jesus intends for us to try, even when things are at such a pass that we no longer want to try at all.

This is my third point (my third sermon!) **In uncertainty we'll find our way together.** If there is anything we, in the late twentieth century, are looking for, it is a sense that something is certain; and if there is anything we can assume, it is uncertainty.

That, in fact, sometimes seems like the only thing that *is* certain: uncertainty! But Jesus said be certain about this: "I will do whatever you ask in my name, so that the Father may be glorified in the Son. If in my name you ask me for anything, I will do it" (John 14:13-14 *NRSV*).

Something else you can be certain about. He didn't mean a word of it; not if you take those words to mean that whatever you want, you'll get, if you ask. Jesus' words do not convey a right to whatever we want.

Charles Cousar writes, "... Jesus makes the pledge to the disciples (repeatedly) that their prayers will be answered. The text makes clear, however, that this pledge is not a willy-nilly commitment to give to overly indulgent children whatever their hearts fancy. Prayers are to be made 'in [Jesus] name', that is, they are to be made out of the disciples' relationship established with and by Jesus. The answering of the requests does not serve those who pray, but is to the end 'that the Father may be glorified in the Son.' These are prayers offered in behalf of the community and the community's mission. They undergird the 'greater works' that the church is to perform."[4]

Right prayer, says Jesus, is for God's glory, not just our aggrandizement. And right prayer is prayed not only with our words, but with our lives.

This week I picked up a story on a computer chat line called "Eculaugh." It's a place where we Christians, who too often fight about things, are encouraged to laugh about things. For those of you into the Internet, the "subject" line reads, "Only Good Clean Religious Humor (all 4) All Else Removed."

This story goes, "There was this guy and he really needed some money, so he got on his knees and he prayed the Lord would bless him by winning the lottery. After the prayer, he gets up and goes

97

about his business. The next day he's on his knees praying again saying, 'Lord, you know I really need this money and to win the lottery would be such a great blessing. Think of all the people I could help with the money. I thought for sure I'd win it yesterday, but I didn't. Please Lord, I'm begging you.' And off he went.

"The next day, he's back on his knees crying out to God, 'Please Lord, I need this money! Is something the matter, God? Why don't you answer my prayer?' Suddenly a voice from Heaven calls out to him, 'Hey! Meet me halfway, would you! Buy a ticket!' "[5]

The moral of the story is not run down to the gas station right after church and God will make you a millionaire by morning. The moral is that what we pray for we need to be willing to work for, and the only answer we need to hear is "Well done! You have done what God wants you to do." Does that get me everything I want? No. But can I be certain of everything I need? You betcha!

In the uncertainties of life and death, *this is certain*: "In life and in death we belong to God ... (and) nothing in life or in death can separate us from the love of God in Christ Jesus our Lord," who calls us together to face life, death, and uncertainty together with him.

---

1. *The Zondervan Parallel New Testament in Greek and English* (Grand Rapids, Michigan: Zondervan Bible Publishers, 1980).

2. Bradley J. Longfield, *The Presbyterian Controversy: Fundamentalists, Modernists and Moderates* (Oxford University Press, November 1,1993), p. 118.

3. Barclay M. Newman and Eugene A. Nida, *A Handbook on The Gospel of John*, UBS Handbook Series (New York: United Bible Societies, 1980), p. 455.

4. C. Cousar, et al., *Texts for Preaching, A Lectionary Commentary Based on the NRSV — Year A* (Louisville, Kentucky: Westminster/John Knox Press, 1995).

5. *Eculaugh* Note 2670.

I Will Not
Leave You Alone

John 14:15-21

There's an old saying about the way you get people to hear what you're saying, that goes something like: Tell them what you're going to tell them. Tell them. Then, tell them what you told them.

For some reason I connect that with the military, but this morning I want to connect that with Jesus. Because the way the writer of the Gospel according to John has set up the teaching of Jesus in the passage I just read is like that. Jesus tells us what he is going to tell us. Jesus tells us. Then Jesus tells us what he told us.

To disciples who were as disconcerted about their lives as we often are about ours, Jesus said: "... I will ask the Father to send you the Holy Spirit who will help you and always be with you" (John 14:16 *CEV*).

What he's telling us he's going to tell us is that he will not leave us alone. Then he tells us: "I won't leave you like orphans. I will come back to you" (John 14:18 *CEV*).

I will not leave you alone!

Don't get hung up right there on theories and theologies about the how and when of what some would call the "second" coming. Because, first, before all that, Jesus is simply telling us what he told us he would tell us.

I will not leave you alone!

And then, like a parent (maybe, today, like a mother) who says to a child, "If I've told you once, I've told you a thousand times!" Jesus tells us what he told us: "The Holy Spirit will come and help you, because the Father will send the Spirit to take my place ... So don't be worried or afraid" (John 14:26-27 *CEV*).

I will not leave you alone!

Where I am, and always will be, is with you. "Rise, let us be on our way" (John 14:31 *NRSV*). "It is time for us to go now" (John 14:31 *CEV*). C'mon — let's go! Whatever happens, we're in it together, said Jesus.

The teaching in John takes us back before the crucifixion, when Jesus' disciples were, perhaps, only beginning to realize the political realities of Jesus' situation. It wasn't any easier than it is for you or me for Jesus to fight "City Hall." It wasn't any easier than it is for you or me for Jesus to stand for right in face of wrong. It wasn't any easier than it is for you or me for Jesus to make hard decisions. And the Bible never tells us it will get easier. What it does tell us is that when it gets harder, we can hold fast to God's promise to be with us and not to leave us hanging out there alone.

Jesus knew full well that those who hang in there sometimes get hung out to dry, and even hung on a cross to die. He is not denying that reality. He is pointing to a greater reality — the presence of God with you and me, knowing full well how hard it is for you and me to hear it.

Jesus was a Jew. To the Jews first, and to all of us always, God has called us to hear what he tells us. The single greatest truth the people of God have proclaimed from the beginning, the great truth of Israel, calls us to hear that God has not abandoned us, that God will never leave us — alone.

Our Jewish friends call it "the Shema" from the Hebrew for "hear." "Hear, O Israel: The Lord is our God, the Lord alone. You shall love the Lord your God with all your heart; and with all your soul; and with all your might" (Deuteronomy 6:4 *NRSV*).

"Listen, Israel! The Lord our God is the only true God! So love the Lord your God with all your heart, soul, and strength" (*CEV*).

That's the faith of Jesus who said to you and me, "Have faith in God and have faith in me."

"... I will ask the Father to send you the Holy Spirit who will help you and always be with you" (John 14:1, 16 *CEV*).

I will not leave you alone!

I just moved biblically from the words of the writer of the ancient book of Deuteronomy to the words of Jesus. I can do that because that's what the Bible does. It tells us what God is going to tell us. It tells us. And it tells us what he told us. From walking in the Garden with God in the book of Genesis, to waking up in heaven with God in the Revelation of John, the Bible says God is with his people, and we are always with him. As the Psalmist put it, "The Lord of hosts is with us" (Psalm 46:7, 11 *NRSV*). "The Lord All-Powerful is with us" (*CEV*). And always will be.

Jesus said that to his disciples who'd heard it before, knowing full well that they didn't hear it — not really. So having told them what they had already been told by their faith in the God of Abraham and Isaac and Jacob, and having told them himself of God's love in him, he told them, "The Spirit will teach you everything and will remind you of what I said..." (John 14:26 *CEV*). The Spirit will tell you what I told you.

This is one of those passages where we have to deal with the Doctrine of the Trinity, our attempt to understand and explain God as God the Father, God the Son, and God the Holy Spirit. This doctrine has vexed Christians from the beginning.

And we've come up with everything from three Gods to a God who is a committee.

But could it be so simple as to take Jesus at his word? That by his revelation of himself as Father, Son, and Holy Spirit, God has simply told us (1), and told us (2), and told us (3) of his love and his presence with us.

On this Chancel Choir Recognition Sunday, we need to hear the words we sing and heed them. We began with these:

> *So has the church,*
> *in liturgy and song,*
> *In faith and love, through centuries of wrong,*
> *Borne witness to the truth in every tongue ...*[1]

The truth by which we can live and die! The Lord of hosts is with us. Jesus Christ is with us. The Holy Spirit, the Lord of hosts, the presence of Christ in the here-and-now is with us — with you and with me.

That's something in which we can take great comfort. It can also be very disconcerting. We have to be careful, lest we turn God into a caretaker whose only concern is keeping you and me comfortable. Someone once said that the job of a pastor is to comfort the afflicted and afflict the comfortable. That, says Jesus, is also the way of God the Holy Spirit.

Now I just told you what I'm going to tell you. So let me tell you. God the Holy Spirit comforts the afflicted and afflicts the comfortable. Now let me tell you what I told you. And I can do that in one word, a Greek word: *parakletos*. When I read it earlier, you heard it from Jesus, translated: "I will ask the Father, and he will send you another *Advocate* — *parakletos* — to be with you forever" (John 14:16 *NRSV*). Some of us memorized that in the *King James Version*: "... I will pray the Father, and he shall give you another *comforter* ..." — *parakletos* (*KJV*).

We typically understand that to mean the Father will send the Holy Spirit to help us out. But English tends to limit our understanding of the role of God's Spirit with us. The *New Revised Standard Version* translates the word as "Advocate" — one who stands up for us, who speaks out for us, who acts on our behalf. And that's fine, as far as it goes. But it doesn't go far enough in telling us what it means to say the *Spirit* of God is with us. Yes, he stands up for us, but the "Paraclete" that Jesus promised is also "the one who comforts" us.[2]

The Greek word *parakletos* also means "the one who exhorts" us.[3] The one who *expects* us to listen, and calls us to account when we don't. If you've got a "guilty conscience" you're hearing the Holy Spirit tell you you can do better, exhorting you to be better.

This "Paraclete," this "Holy Spirit," is no heavenly happy hour, but rather, God, the Father Almighty, Creator of heaven and earth, who holds us, and helps us, and comforts us, and stands up for us, *and holds us accountable* — and exhorts us to do the same for each other. To do the same for each other is to do what Jesus said, when he said, "If you love me, you will do as I command. Then I will ask the Father to send you the Holy Spirit who will help you and always be with you" (John 14:15 *CEV*).

What he's telling you is he'll be there for you even when it seems in what you do you're all alone. If you believe that, then you can live that.

G. K. Chesterton, in *What's Wrong with the World*, wrote, "The Christian ideal has not been tried and found wanting. It has been found difficult; and left untried."

The Holy Spirit exhorts us, challenges us, prods us, encourages us to try, in the knowledge that in our trying we are not alone.

The Indian leader Gandhi, in being persecuted by those he sought to help, sang an Indian poem that goes, "If they answer not your call, walk alone, walk alone."[4]

And there are times when life feels that way. But there is never a time when we are truly alone. The Lord of hosts, our Lord Jesus Christ, the Spirit of the Lord is with us.

Jesus said, "I obey my Father, so that everyone in the world might know that I love him." Then he said, "It is time for us to go now" (John 14:31 *CEV*). It is time for us to go and live — and die — what we believe: that what we've been told — and told — and told — is true.

---

1. Fred P. Green, "When In Our Music God Is Glorified," *The Presbyterian Hymnal*, no. 264 (Louisville, Kentucky: Westminster/John Knox Press).

2. *The New Interpreter's Bible, Volume IX* (Nashville, Tennessee: John Abingdon Press, 1995), p. 747.

3. *Ibid.*

4. Quoted in *Christianity Today*, 4/22/83t.

He Ascended
Into Heaven

Luke 24:44-53

I want to take the text seriously this morning. It would be easy not to, because Luke's story of the ascension of Jesus is not easy no matter how you take it. For you and me, twenty centuries later, this story may be very hard to take very seriously.

Our take on the ascension of Jesus might be on the order of liturgy as lift-off: Jesus being lifted up to the Air Force song: "Off we go into the wild blue yonder, climbing high into the sky!"

Or we might take this as a story that defines worship as wondering where Jesus went and our lives as wondering where he is when we need him!

Maybe we take it to mean our faith is fairly far-fetched. Not only did he get up from the grave, he levitated out of life, at least as we live it, grounded as we are in the realities of life. Realities that do more to weight us down with worry, than to send us soaring up through the skies.

On this Ascension Sunday when we're recognizing all those who have worked so hard this past year to make programs happen here at church, and we're giving each of them a balloon, I couldn't help but think, if you could just get enough of those together, if you and I could just get it together, could we be lifted, like Mary Poppins, above our distress into the peace and the presence of God? Could our lives lift off with all the peace and tranquility of a hot air balloon that lifts into the summer sky with barely a whisper?

I'm going to be at the General Assembly of our denomination in Albuquerque, New Mexico, this summer. Balloonists call it "hot air heaven." They tell me that in addition to the hot air at the General

Assembly, there will be plenty of opportunities for hot air balloon rides. I hope to try it. I'd like to see how that feels. Just for once, to just stand there and "be lifted up."

Somewhere in my files there is an article from *The Wall Street Journal* that describes a church in California where the pastor lifts off regularly — all jokes about "hot air" aside. From time to time, in a moment of great drama, as only in California, his pulpit is enveloped in smoke and flames and high tech pyrotechnics, and it rises, with him aboard, through the ceiling of the sanctuary, where, I presume, he gets out in the attic, climbs over light fixtures and ceiling supports, and comes back down to earth with the rest of us.

Life is like that. Even when something gives us a lift, it doesn't last — for long. It doesn't last long enough. And we're left wondering, like the disciples who watched Jesus go, "What happened!?"

What happened to my hopes and dreams? What happened to my great expectations? What happened to my marriage, my career, my kids, my country, my community, what I've counted on all my life? What happened to me?

Those are the kinds of questions that don't always make you feel high and lifted up. Those are the kinds of questions that can leave you feeling hopeless and left behind. Like the disciples of Jesus who, having seen him die, and then saw him alive again after the resurrection, now saw him leave as he was "lifted up ... into heaven" (Acts 1:9, 11).

I think the "lift-off" was the least of it. What the disciples saw going up in smoke, like a cloud, were their hopes and dreams, and everything to which they had committed their lives. It says they just stood there gazing into nothingness — no doubt with their mouths open. And I have to wonder, if CNN had been there, what they'd have had to say.

The Scottish theologian William Barclay had this to say about this event: "The ascension is far and away the most difficult incident in the life of Jesus either to visualize or to understand ... No one has ever succeeded in painting a picture of the ascension which was anything other than grotesque and ridiculous. In films of the life of Christ, if the ascension is portrayed, the whole matter descends into sheer bathos."[1]

I looked up "bathos" in the dictionary. It means "ludicrous, trite, or mawkishly sentimental." But I think the ascension is more serious than that, and we need to take it seriously.

It's serious enough that we regularly say we believe it. The Apostles' Creed says that among all the other things I say I believe, I say I believe "he ascended into heaven." And the writer of the Gospel of Luke and the Book of Acts, same writer, thought it was serious enough to say it twice.

He said it first as the conclusion to his Gospel, that we call Luke; and then at the beginning of his sequel, that we call Acts. Whatever happened that day, for Luke it sums up the gospel, and it sets the stage for things to come.

In a sense, first, **Ascension sums up the gospel.** You might say it makes the resurrection mean something. That the good news we call the "gospel" truth is not just that Jesus *was raised* from the dead, but that he *is risen* to new life. If Jesus had only been raised from the dead he could have died again.

He could have just ridden off into the sunset after a long run that ran out. He could have simply turned up missing, or snuck off when no one was looking.

The power of the resurrection comes in saying that he "ascended into heaven," and that as the men in white said to disbelieving disciples, *believe it*, "... he will come back ..." (Acts 1:11 *CEV*); believe it, "... he will come to judge the living and the dead" (The Apostles' Creed, Ecumenical).

Believe it; he is alive forever, and as he said, "Because I live, you also will live" (John 14:19 *NRSV*).

Resurrection is not just resuscitation; it is being raised to life forever, lifted up into life as God means it to be for you and me.

As Harold Daniels, of our denomination's office of worship down the road in Louisville, has put it, "Ascension day marks the assumption of glory and power by the crucified and risen Lord ... Ascension day embodies the meaning of the Easter season ... (Ascension day means) Jesus Christ is Lord!"

Reaching for a way to say what that means, the church has reached back to the Psalms:

Clap your hands, all you peoples;
shout to God with loud songs of joy.
For the LORD, the Most High, is awesome,
a great king over all the earth.
God has gone up with a shout,
the LORD with the sound of a trumpet.

— Psalm 47:1-2, 5-7

Ascension says that Jesus Christ is Lord.

But that just **sets the stage for what's to come**, because, as Beverly Gaventa writes, that's the least of it! She says: "While the liturgical tradition of the church has tended to make the ascension of Jesus into a festival to his glory and power, the emphasis in the biblical tradition is elsewhere ... The interest in Acts 1 appears to be less in what is happening to Jesus than in what is about to happen in the lives of the earliest Christians."[2]

As spectacular as whatever happened may have been, however "California" it may sound, the emphasis that Luke is putting on it is not as much on what happened to Jesus as on what was beginning to happen to the disciples. Not so much on Jesus "going," as on God "coming," as the Holy Spirit, into the lives of that very dispirited group of folks we know as the first Christ followers — "first Christians."

Twice Luke has Jesus promising that though he would be absent *from* them, God the Holy Spirit would be present *with* them. And don't get all hyper about the "Holy Spirit." (Presbyterians do!) It's just a way of saying the presence of God. Simply put, Jesus' going would not mean that God was gone.

It's no accident, I think, that Luke immediately lists those whose lives had been affected. As though to say to them, and to you and me, that "God the father almighty, creator of heaven and earth," Jesus Christ, our risen and ascended Lord, is still the Lord of people like "... Peter, and John, and James, and Andrew, Philip and Thomas, Bartholomew and Matthew, James son of Alphaeus, and Simon the Zealot, and Judas son of James ... (and of) certain women, including Mary the mother of Jesus, as well as his brothers" (Acts 1:13-14 *NRSV*).

They'd ridden an emotional and spiritual roller coaster with Jesus. Those are the people who loved Jesus in life, mourned him in death, believed in his resurrection, and lost sight of him at "ascension." Cedar Point Amusement Park aside, that had to be the most harrowing roller coaster ride in history.

On a modern psychological stress test those folks were off the charts, if not by this point off the wall, as many would claim. They were right where you and I are sometimes. Right where we least want to be. And right there is where they discovered the presence of God. No pie-in-the-sky, no piece-of-cake, just the peace that comes when we can say with Paul, as we Presbyterians do:

> *I am convinced that neither death, nor life, nor angels, nor rulers, nor things present, nor things to come, nor powers, nor height, nor depth, nor anything else in all creation, will be able to separate us from the love of God in Christ Jesus our Lord* — Romans 8:38-39 *NRSV*

The same Jesus "(who) rose again from the dead, ... **ascended into heaven**, and sitteth on the right hand of God the Father Almighty; (who) from thence ... shall come ..." to you and me.

---

1. William Barclay, *The Apostles' Creed for Everyman* (New York and Evanston: Harper & Row, Publishers, 1967).

2. B. Gaventa, et al, *Texts for Preaching, A Lectionary Commentary Based on the NRSV — Year A* (Louisville, Kentucky: Westminster/John Knox Press, 1995), p. 311.

What Jesus Prayed For

John 17:1-11

What do you pray for? Maybe the question should be: "Do you pray?!"

But let's assume that sometime, somewhere, somehow, everybody prays; that as someone with the voice of experience once said, "There are no atheists in foxholes." There are no "non-prayers" when the only thing left to do is pray.

So, whenever you do pray, **whatever do you pray *for*?**

I have prayed for the patience of my editor as I worked on completing this book of sermons. So far my prayer has been answered. But I ran across this prayer recently, and I might just pray it, too. It's dubbed "the prayer of an author."

> *Grant, I beseech thee, O God, that all who read this book may be conscious of the deep spiritual insight of the writer; that the sale of this book may result in a nice little nest egg; that copies of this book, nicely bound, may make an impressive sight on the bookshelf; (and) that amid all the congratulatory applause, the writer may remain conspicuously humble.* — Source unknown

But whether I pray that or not, what I want to know, really, what I want you to know for yourself is: **What do *you* pray for?** Another way to put it is: **What do you want?** What do you want out of life? What do you want out of God? What do you want badly enough that you'll talk to the ceiling (or to the floor) to get it? Whether you raise your face to see if God is there, or lower your

111

head in fear he might be, or in deference if he happens to be, what do you ask, what do you say, when you pray?

Our Associate Pastor, John Wurster, likes to alphabetize things. I thought I'd try it.

Do you pray for **A**ffluence, a **B**ig **B**ank **B**alance, a new **C**ar, or a new **D**irection for your life? How about an **E**asier life for you or someone you love? Some people seem to want a **F**ree ride! Someone once said that around stewardship time in church it looks like a lot of folks expect to go to heaven on a scholarship! So do you ever pray for increased **G**enerosity? (And not just for someone else, but for you, too?)

Some people pray to go to **H**eaven, out of fear God will get them and they'll go to **H**ell. I know folks who pray because they're **I**nsecure, including some folks who look and sound anything but.

Just one more chance is what some prayers are prayed for. **J**ust one more chance with my kids, my spouse, my parents, my job, my life. Some people pray to be **K**ept safe and secure. Others to be **L**et **L**oose from suffocating security. **M**oney is always on some people's list. And the prayer is always for **M**ore.

No more of whatever it is that's driving me **N**uts gets prayed for a lot. New **O**pportunities, new **P**ossibilities, answers to old **Q**uestions, and **R**elief from old **R**egrets, all get mentioned. Some of us pray for **S**omething **S**ecret down deep in our **S**ouls we've never shared with anyone.

Terrible things get lots of attention. Anybody paying attention to this world of ours, knows we have a lot praying to do.

The **U**sual things get prayed about. They're on everyone's list and they should be: sickness, suffering, sadness, circumstances beyond our control.

We pray for **V**ictory for the good, in **W**ar with the bad, as a nation, as concerned parents, in our neighborhoods, on our streets. We pray for e**X**cellence (I cheated!). We pray for **Y**et another chance. We pray for **Z**ZZZ's, because everything else we pray for keeps us awake at night. **A** to **Z**. We pray. Sometime, somewhere, somehow, we pray.

And when we can't pray? Well then, the Scriptures say, Christ prays *for* us — not just about us but on behalf of us, when we can't pray.

That doesn't mean we shouldn't pray for ourselves or for others, but that we have more going for us than we might think. Even when we might be thinking in our praying of giving up.

I'm a great lover of mystery stories, and especially the stories of Dame Agatha Christie. But there's no mystery in how we need to live. We need to pray. And we need to "never, never, never, give up."

Winston Churchill said that. Dame Agatha said this. She told this story in her autobiography. It's about frogs. But it's really about what it means to lead a prayerful life which is more than just mouthing a lot of prayers.

> *It seems two frogs jumped into a bucket of cream on a dairy farm. "May as well give up," croaked one after trying in vain to get out. "We're goners!" "Keep on paddling," said the other frog. "We'll get out of this mess somehow!" "It's no use," said the first. "Too thick to swim. Too thin to jump. Too slippery to crawl. We're bound to die sometime anyway, so it may as well be tonight." He sank to the bottom of the bucket and died.*
>
> *His friend just kept on paddling, and paddling, and paddling.* (And probably praying and praying and praying.) *By morning he was perched on a mass of butter that he had churned all by himself. There he was, with a grin on his face, eating the flies that came swarming from every direction.*[1]

Prayer is about not giving up on yourself or on God.

The prayer Jesus prayed was prayed at a time when giving up would have been easy. Jesus prayed his prayer between dinner and death. Between having dinner with his disciples (one of whom would deny him, all of whom would desert him, and one of whom would do him in) and dealing with the political realities that would lead to his death, **Jesus prayed.** But he did not pray for a way out; he prayed for a way forward. What Jesus prayed for when his praying time was running short was not what you'd expect. Not that long list I made.

He prayed first that in what was happening to him God would be glorified. We pray like that when we pray like him: "Our Father who art in heaven, hallowed be your name ..." "Glorified be your name." He told us to pray that first. In all the rest of the stuff I've got to talk to you about, God, may there be some glory in all this for you.

Then he prayed for his disciples. He prayed for those he loved. He prayed, "Father, I don't ask you to take my followers out of the world, but keep them safe ..." (John 17:15 *CEV*).

The great preacher Phillips Brooks once said, "Do not pray for tasks equal to your powers. Pray for powers equal to your tasks" (Source unknown). That's what Jesus prayed for his disciples. Power to handle the problems ahead.

But he also prayed for something else. Something important for us to hear. He prayed it for the disciples. And he prayed it for you and me. And he was rather insistent about it. It was the last part of the last line I read from the lesson. He prayed: "... that they may be one, as we are one" (John 17:11 *NRSV*). "We" was Jesus and God. "They" were Jesus' closest friends. Jesus prayed for his friends a closeness, a sense of in-it-together-ness, a reality of oneness like that of God and himself.

And he also prayed that for you and me. In the part of the prayer we didn't read Jesus prayed: "I ask ... that they may all be one" (John 17:21 *NRSV*). "... that they may be one, as we are one" (John 17:22 *NRSV*). "... that they may become completely one" (John 17:23 *NRSV*). Three times in three sentences Jesus prayed that you and I might be of one mind and one spirit — the mind and spirit of God.

Most on Jesus' mind and in Jesus' prayers the night before he died was you and me, and whether you and I would get it together. So we could go-it-together through that list of things we've all got. Whether people like you and me would ever come to understand that we're in-it-together whether we like it or not. That that's the way life is. And that the way to live life is not "every man for himself," but "all-for-one and one-for-all." That's two clichés in one sentence. So be it. It's true. And that's what Jesus prayed for.

That which divides us is that which destroys us. Jesus knew it — it was destroying him. Be it the color of our skin, the color of our money, or the subdivisions in which we live, division will do us in.

So, in the urgency of that time between dinner and death, Jesus prayed that we would not be divided.He prayed that we would be one — nd not just with each other, but with him. The sense of oneness Christ prayed for us with each other is the same oneness he prays for us to have with God. There's a vertical relationship between God and me and a horizontal relationship between you and me and they should be — in Christ will be — the same. Just think what a world this would be if my relationship with God were like Jesus' relationship with God, and that was mirrored in my relationship with everyone around me.

This was no *prima donna* prayer though. Jesus' prayer for the safety of his friends says so. But still he prayed for what still seems impossible: that the kind of love we see in the relationship Jesus had with God would be the kind of love in all the relationships of our lives. Was he asking too much? It might seem so. But he didn't think so. That's why he prayed for it.

As I read Jesus' prayer, I thought about a prayer I've prayed a hundred times. I think I've prayed it at every wedding I've ever done. It's part of the prayer for the new couple — a word which itself means "coupling," or putting together, or making one.

It goes: "Grant that their wills may be so knit together in your will, and their spirits in your Spirit, that they may grow in love and peace with you and each other all the days of their life."[2]

Does it always happen? No. But that's what Jesus prayed for you and me, the night before he died for you and me: that what he knew we couldn't do, God would do. He prayed God would make us one with each other and with him. That means you and I can pray no less.

We sing no less. The hymn says:

> *In Christ there is no east or west,*
> *In him no south or north;*
> *But one great fellowship of love*
> *Through-out the whole wide earth.*[3]

We sing it. Jesus prayed we'd learn to live it — right here where we live together.

1. Agatha Christie, *Autobiography.*

2. *Book of Common Worship*, p. 848.

3. John Oxenham, "In Christ There is No East Or West," *The Presbyterian Hymnal*, no. 439 (Louisville, Kentucky: Westminster/John Knox Press).

Books In This Cycle A Series

GOSPEL SET
And Then Came The Angel
Sermons for Advent/Christmas/Epiphany
William B. Kincaid, III

The Lord Is Risen! He Is Risen Indeed! He Really Is!
Sermons For Lent/Easter
Richard L. Sheffield

No Post-Easter Slump
Sermons For Sundays After Pentecost (First Third)
Wayne H. Keller

We Walk By Faith
Sermons For Sundays After Pentecost (Middle Third)
Richard Gribble

Where Gratitude Abounds
Sermons For Sundays After Pentecost (Last Third)
Joseph M. Freeman

FIRST LESSON SET
Between Gloom And Glory
Sermons For Advent/Christmas/Epiphany
R. Glen Miles

Cross, Resurrection, And Ascension
Sermons For Lent/Easter
Richard Gribble

Is Anything Too Wonderful For The Lord?
Sermons For Sundays After Pentecost (First Third)
Leonard W. Mann

The Divine Salvage
Sermons For Sundays After Pentecost (Middle Third)
R. Curtis and Tempe Fussell

When God Says, "Let Me Alone"
Sermons For Sundays After Pentecost (Last Third)
William A. Jones

SECOND LESSON SET
Moving At The Speed Of Light
Sermons For Advent/Christmas/Epiphany
Frank Luchsinger

Love Is Your Disguise
Sermons For Lent/Easter
Frank Luchsinger